C000063255

Be the best

How to become a world-class health and safety professional

Richard Byrne

All rights reserved. No part of this publication may be reproduced in any material form (including photocopying or storing it in any medium by electronic or photographic means and whether or not transiently or incidentally to some other use of this publication) without written permission of the copyright owner. Applications for written permission to reproduce any part of this publication should be addressed to the publisher, IOSH Services Limited.

IOSH and IOSH Services Limited assume no responsibility for the contents of this book, in whole or in part, nor for the interpretation or concepts advanced by the author. The views expressed in this book are the author's own, and do not necessarily reflect those of any employing or other organisation. All web addresses are current at the time of going to press. The publisher takes no responsibility for subsequent changes.

Warning: The doing of an unauthorised act in relation to a copyright work may result in both a civil claim for damages and criminal prosecution.

Richard Byrne has asserted his right under the Copyright, Designs and Patents Act 1988 to be identified as the author of this work.

Published 2009

© Richard Byrne 2009
Printed in England by the Lavenham Press Limited

ISBN 978 0 901357 45 8

Published by IOSH Services Ltd
The Grange
Highfield Drive
Wigston
Leicestershire
LE18 1NN
UK
t +44 (0)116 257 3100
f +44 (0)116 257 3101
www.iosh.co.uk

Contents

About the author

Richard Byrne graduated from Aston University in 2001 with a first-class combined honours degree in ergonomics and health and safety management. Since then, he's worked in health and safety at the Midlands Co-operative Society, Royal Mail Group and Wolseley UK. His experiences have also taken him into the much broader area of corporate social responsibility.

He's a Chartered Member of IOSH and an Associate Member of the Institute of Environmental Management and Assessment, and holds the European Occupational Safety and Health Manager accreditation. Richard has written numerous feature articles for health and safety periodicals and is an examiner for the National Examination Board in Occupational Safety and Health's National Diploma.

Richard is the Group Health, Safety and Environmental Manager for ATS Euromaster and lives with his family in Staffordshire.

Acknowledgments

First of all, I'd like to thank my family for their ever-continuing love, support and belief.

I'd also like to extend my thanks to Irene Stark, Group Human Resources Director at ATS Euromaster, for allowing me the chance to explore this opportunity, and the IOSH Publishing team, in particular Caroline Patel and Alex Cameron.

Finally, it would be remiss of me not to thank Tony Higgins for giving a young safety graduate a chance and keeping him on the straight and narrow, while allowing him the opportunities to deal with things that many people never get a shot at in their whole career.

Introduction

This isn't a typical health and safety book, as it won't tell you why you should manage health and safety, or even what you should be managing – there are enough of those around already! Instead, it explores various tools and techniques that help with the 'how' of managing it.

Take, for example, the topic of health and safety auditing and inspection. From a technical point of view, we know these activities are critical. But when you have limited resources, how do you go about implementing a robust audit programme and still do all the other things you have to do?

It's true that we do learn a little of the 'how' through our training, but this tends to emphasise the traditional methods, such as using safety posters to help spread a message. This is a good start and will get you so far. But 'so far' isn't enough these days, particularly as any organisation worth its salt is looking for continual improvement, against the backdrop of very tough economic and market conditions. And of course the safety professional's role is a management one, so we should be managing!

One of my main drivers for writing this book was born out of my personal frustration with the public stereotypes of our profession. Let's face it – when you're asked in the pub what you do for a living and you say 'health and safety', one of two things generally happen. Either the person you're talking to has a major gripe about the subject and spends the next half hour telling you how it's all 'your' fault, or the conversation stops dead!

Another factor was my experience of interviewing candidates for safety positions and meeting other safety professionals. In these contexts, I've been struck by the gap that exists between getting the qualification and actually being useful and competent in the subject.

So for me there were two choices: either put up and shut up, or write this book.

None of what you'll read in this book is rocket science. It shouldn't be, because if health and safety is going to work, it needs to be simple. As a great safety professional I am indebted to once told me: "It should make business slicker, smarter, faster."

I've aimed to avoid including too much theory because my intention is that this book should be full of practical ideas – a tool kit if you like –

that you can dip in and out of as you need to. The central theme is that safety professionals need to be more commercially 'savvy' and business-focused to achieve their goals in the modern workplace.

The chapters can be grouped into four main areas. The first three chapters explore where health and safety has come from, where it's going in the context of the 21st century organisation and, crucially, the huge opportunity this presents.

We all know that we should have a health and safety strategy in place that is clearly linked to the organisation's overall aims and objectives as well as management systems that help people manage safely. We also know that 'death by PowerPoint' doesn't make a 'sexy' training course and that auditing arrangements are important, although not the be-all and end-all. But how do we do it? The next four chapters are dedicated to exploring these issues and offering some solutions.

Chapter 8, on overcoming inaction, is particularly important. Some years ago at university, we covered something called 'systems thinking'. If I'm honest, I didn't really get it at the time, as it seemed too abstract. It was only when I started working in management roles that it all made sense. I've tried to use this way of thinking in this chapter to help look at the problem of inaction in a different way. It does take a little effort to get your head round it, but once you do, the results speak for themselves.

The final chapters explore some tools and techniques to help you engage with the three main workplace populations: directors and senior managers, middle management and front line managers, and employees. These techniques have been exploited by many organisations for some time, and having used most of them myself, I've tweaked them in places to reflect my experience – which is another way of saying that you can learn from my mistakes!

I hope that you find this book useful and thought-provoking. Of course, I welcome your feedback, which can be addressed to the publishers.

EurOSHM Richard Byrne
BSc (Hons) CMIOSH AIEMA
December 2009

Chapter 1: Clipboard and cagoule

The general perception the public holds of the health and safety profession is one of people wandering around the workplace with a clipboard, wearing a cagoule and saying "You can't do that." Or at least that's what the media would have you believe.

Sometimes we as a profession don't help ourselves, though. Take, for example, the way we've traditionally publicised what we do. How do we do it? We publicise the number of workplace accidents there've been. In other words, we almost set ourselves up to fail by spreading bad news. That's not to say that raising the profile of the number of accidents in the workplace is wrong, because there is a place for it. But we need to sell ourselves more to the public and to businesses – we need to show that we add value. Quite simply, perception is reality.

In this chapter we'll explore the public's perception of the safety profession, as understanding this view is vital to help 'break the mould' and add real value to business in the 21st century. The later chapters will offer some answers and solutions to the challenges we face.

A potted history of health and safety in the UK
Health and safety has always been with us in some form or another. Although you may never have considered it in this way before, take for example our medieval ancestors. They tried to avoid harm by wearing armour and using shields when they went into battle.

The first piece of legislation relating to health and safety at work was the Health and Morals of Apprentices Act, introduced in 1802. This Act specified some minimum working and living standards for children working in mills, and required them to be given a basic education.

Later in the 19th century a series of Factory Acts was passed and the first factory inspectors were introduced, no doubt amid much resistance from employers. Health and safety legislation continued in much the same prescriptive manner until the introduction of the Health and Safety at Work etc Act in 1974.

This Act was a complete reversal of the existing approach and changed the way industry viewed health and safety. While the new legislation outlined in general terms what employers had to do to safeguard their employees and others, it didn't tell them what to do in every situation. In other words, the message was clear: "It's your business. Manage it how you see fit, but if you get it wrong, the comeback will be severe."

This change from a prescriptive to a goal-setting approach was critical. It was the idea of Lord Robens and the committee he chaired in 1972. The Robens committee found that there was too much apathy towards health and safety. It also discovered that those businesses that took health and safety seriously and really engaged with the subject tended to be more prosperous than those that followed the rules simply because they had to, or didn't follow them at all.[1]

Since the introduction of the Health and Safety at Work etc Act, a number of statutory instruments have been passed by Parliament to support it. These either enact European Union legislation or clarify the general instructions given by the 1974 Act. For example, the Workplace (Health, Safety and Welfare) Regulations 1992 were introduced as a result of a European Directive, but also add meat to the bones of the general duties of the Health and Safety at Work etc Act, especially by being more specific about safe pedestrian and vehicle routes and providing welfare facilities.

It's a little ironic that the introduction of regulations such as these means that health and safety law is becoming more prescriptive. Even so, the statistics on deaths, injuries and ill health at work suggest that this tactic is having a positive effect. It also makes the law clearer for organisations that are unsure about what they need to do and easier for a court to convict when employers fail in their duties.

Since 1974, there've been two pieces of health and safety legislation that can be seen as major landmarks. In 1992, the so-called 'six-pack' of EU-inspired regulations was introduced. The most influential of these were the Management of Health and Safety at Work Regulations (updated in 1999), which saw the risk assessment process spelled out for everyone and cemented risk assessment as the backbone of modern health and safety management. While some previous legislation required risk assessments in certain specific circumstances, the Management Regulations introduced the universal requirement for general assessments.

More recently, in 2007 the Corporate Manslaughter and Corporate Homicide Act was brought in to make prosecution easier where fatal accidents occur and to prevent organisations citing the lack of a 'directing mind' when something goes wrong.

Too much red tape

Since the introduction of the first version of the Reporting of Injuries, Diseases and Dangerous Occurrences Regulations (RIDDOR) in 1985, the Health and Safety Executive (HSE) has recorded the number of fatal accidents, major injuries and accidents that have prevented the injured person from working for more than three days. These figures are shown in the graph on the next page, along with a timeline of health and safety legislation.

The 1974 Act and the Regulations that have been made since are accompanied by numerous guidance documents. In its 2008 catalogue,[2] HSE Books lists around 130 publications in the General Occupational Health and Safety series, 76 in the Legal series, and about 105 guidance notes. This may seem like a lot of paperwork to get your head around, but it's a vast improvement on the situation that Lord Robens found when he started his research in 1970. At that time, there were reportedly nine main groups of laws, including a staggering 500 subordinate statutory instruments.[1]

While the overall trend in the accident data presented in the graph overleaf suggests that the number of work-related fatal accidents and major and over-three-day injuries is decreasing, without detailed research it's difficult to prove that this is a result of introducing additional legislation. In other words, there are two opposing views on this.

The first is quite simplistic: there's a declining trend because the new legislation is having the desired effect. On one hand, employers are managing risk better through fear of prosecution and, on the other, the additional laws, along with their guidance and codes of practice, make it clearer to employers what they should be doing.

The second view is more complex. It dwells less on simple cause and effect and suggests that the improving trend is linked to other factors, such as the 'good neighbour principle' – where big companies use their influence to encourage improvements elsewhere in the supply chain.

While this may be a rather simplistic overview, on balance, the improved figures probably stem from a mixture of these inputs. Each view has its merits, depending on what access you have to health and safety advice and the type and size of your business.

A media frenzy

Although workplace safety performance in British industry seems to be improving, there's a downside to the higher profile of health and safety. It

The total number of fatal, major and over-three-day accident reports to all relevant populations made to all enforcing authorities between 1986/87 and 2006/07,[4] with a timeline of the introduction of key health and safety legislation. The dashed line shows the overall trend in the data

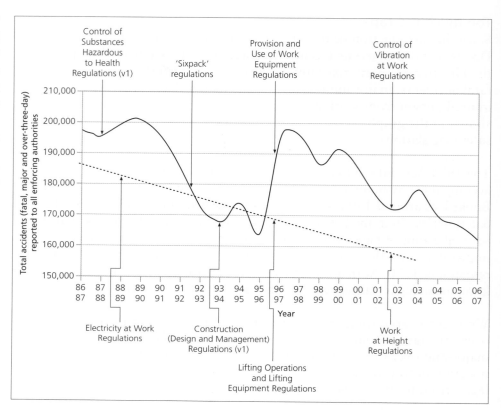

seems that hardly a week goes by without a story appearing in the media about 'health and safety gone mad'. Activities are banned or cancelled, or over-the-top control measures are put in place to deal with trivial or unrealistic risks. It's stories like these that promote the 'clipboard and cagoule' stereotype.

It's difficult to pinpoint exactly when the increase in these stories started. It's undeniable, though, that some comments in the media have helped blow many of them out of proportion.

One famous story involves a headmaster who reportedly asked children at his school to wear safety goggles while playing conkers. The risk of injury from flying conker shards is trivially low – and thus the phrase 'bonkers conkers' entered the health and safety lexicon.

A more recent case concerned the traditional Pancake Race in the Yorkshire city of Ripon. The event was cancelled in 2008, apparently because of the number of risk assessments required by the insurance companies.[3]

It's easy to see why stories like these made the headlines – news editors want good stories and unfortunately these have all the necessary ingredients. They're easy to understand, topical and have a human interest angle. Possibly more importantly, they're controversial and contain an element of bad news – in other words, they're likely to make people tut and ask: "What's the world coming to?"

In most cases, we can feel some sympathy for the people who made the bad decisions. After all, they acted with the best intentions and didn't want to get things wrong on purpose.

There are, of course, a number of reasons for people making bad decisions. Often they feel they have to do something or otherwise they may be criticised (in other words, the problem is self-perpetuating). There can also be a problem with the health and safety advice they base their decisions on. Too often they don't get competent advice because they don't know where to go for it or they get it from an unreliable source.

There are other reasons too. Sometimes, organisations don't want to do something and, rather than saying so, they look for a convenient scapegoat – health and safety. It takes some courage to argue against a policy that supposedly promotes health and safety, so the organisations get their way without the negative publicity that would accompany an announcement of their real reasons for cancelling or banning an event or activity.

As with the Ripon Pancake Race, insurance companies may offer the necessary cover only if extra control measures are taken. If the organisation considers them too onerous or costly, it cites health and safety as the reason for the cancellation. Again, it's possible to see the situation from the insurer's point of view: they're trying to reduce the chances of a major pay-out.

Despite all this, safety professionals may be responsible for some of the bad decisions. Experience has shown that those new to the profession (ie newly qualified) occasionally lack balance in their approach as they tend to focus on the textbook response. Unfortunately, real-life situations don't tend to be covered in a textbook, as each organisation and situation will have its own unique characteristics. It's important to remember that a health and safety qualification gets you 'through the door' and the textbook only provides general principles for reference. Experience and continuing professional development are critical in making sure you're competent.

Sensible risk management

The phrase 'so far as reasonably practicable' was introduced by the Health and Safety at Work etc Act. It enshrines in law the principle that measures taken to deal with safety problems should not be disproportionate to them – in other words, they should be sensible.

Unfortunately, the sensible safety message has got a little confused, which may be one of the reasons for the bad press discussed on the previous page. In response, the Health and Safety Commission (now merged with the HSE) published a statement to help remind people what sensible risk management is all about and what it isn't – there's a summary in the table opposite.

The health and safety community

The 'health and safety community' goes beyond the obvious safety and occupational health professionals and union safety representatives. There are many other influential stakeholders, each with a different reason for being interested. Some internal stakeholders are shown in the table below opposite, along with the potential areas of overlap between their spheres of work and health and safety.

We haven't included the board of directors as a body in the table. Instead, we've presumed that each director will typically be concerned with the health and safety aspects of their departments. They, along with the chief executive or managing director, are also responsible for the organisation's broader approach to corporate social responsibility (CSR) – see Chapter 2.

There are external stakeholders too, who have a similar or sometimes greater influence than those in the organisation. For example:

- shareholders
- enforcing authorities
- customers and suppliers
- insurers
- trade associations.

Conclusion

There's a tendency for people to work in 'silos', and safety professionals are no exception. For us to add value and help deliver world-class safety performance, we need to see the bigger picture in terms of the overall organisational set-up, other business functions and the techniques we use to achieve our aims.

Sensible risk management *is* about:	Sensible risk management *is not* about:
• Ensuring that workers and the public are properly protected • Providing overall benefit to society by balancing benefits and risks, with a focus on reducing real risks – both those which arise more often and those with serious consequences • Enabling innovation and learning, not stifling them • Ensuring that those who create risks manage them responsibly and understand that failure to manage real risks responsibly is likely to lead to robust action • Enabling individuals to understand that as well as the right to protection, they also have to exercise responsibility	• Creating a totally risk-free society • Generating useless paperwork mountains • Scaring people by exaggerating or publicising trivial risks • Stopping important recreational and learning activities for individuals where the risks are managed • Reducing protection of people from risks that cause real harm and suffering

Principles of sensible risk management[5]

Stakeholder	Areas of interest in health and safety topics
Human resources	• Terms and conditions of employment • Employee retention • Sickness absence • Disability discrimination issues • Stress at work • Engagement • Employee and management development • Drug and alcohol misuse programmes
Finance	• Controlling costs • Return on investment
Sales and marketing	• Competitive advantage • Marketing tool
Property/facilities	• Resolution of estate-related problems
Operations	• Reducing days lost due to accidents • Well-defined and workable processes and procedures • Solutions to problems that are 'fit for purpose' and proportionate to the risk
Employees	• Consultation • Engagement • Development • Processes and procedures that don't slow down the job

Internal stakeholders and some areas of interest between their sphere of work and that of the safety professional

The real crux of a modern safety professional's role is to devise a programme that develops a positive safety culture – one where everyone is engaged in working safely. Often, in our keenness to do this, we can go a little overboard and have the opposite effect.

The paradox of health and safety is that you're only as good as the last accident. When everything's going well, you tend to go unnoticed and then questions are asked about what you're doing and whether you're really needed. The trick is to develop other methods and performance indicators to show that safety professionals add value to the organisations they support and are key to helping to meet the organisation's overall objectives. We're not just there for when accidents occur and we need to make sure everyone else realises this.

It's perhaps inevitable that the safety function in an organisation will always have fewer members of staff than other functions that are traditionally seen as central to meeting core objectives. While more resources would undoubtedly make things easier, it's possible to achieve high levels of performance if you 'think outside the box' in what you do and how you do it.

Health and safety shouldn't be about stopping anything. The challenge is to find a way to manage the risks posed by an activity in a sensible way. We've still a long way to go: while the decline in accidents in the last few decades is very welcome, there are still too many people being killed, injured or made ill through work.

Chapter 2: The bigger picture – corporate social responsibility

In the past, health and safety, ethical purchasing, fair pay and diversity were unlikely to be mentioned in the same meeting, let alone the same sentence. But the tide has turned in recent years, with corporate social responsibility (CSR) moving up the agenda, driven by the government and the media. Long gone are the days when the health and safety department worked in isolation. Today's health and safety professional now collaborates with a range of other experts to deliver a holistic CSR programme.

This chapter explores how health and safety professionals fit into the modern organisational set-up, the synergies between what they do and other specialisms, and the opportunities this creates for health and safety.

The bigger picture

CSR has been around for a while but arguably had little impact, except in large, more forward-thinking companies, until the introduction in the UK of the Companies Act in 2006. This places general duties on company directors[6] to:

- consider the interests of their employees in business decision-making
- develop business relationships with suppliers and customers
- consider the impact of their operations on the environment and the community they operate in
- think about maintaining a reputation for high standards of business conduct.

In addition, the Act also requires quoted companies, through their directors' annual report, to provide a review of how the business is managing its obligations to its employees, the environment and the community. These provisions, which are almost hidden in the Act, form the basis of the CSR agenda.

In a nutshell, CSR is about doing the right thing. Companies have been doing the right thing by their shareholders for years: delivering profit and, in turn, good dividends. But these days it's also about how you get there. In other words, you need to do the right thing by *all* stakeholders:

employees, suppliers, customers and the communities your organisation operates in, both in the UK and beyond. The key components that make up the CSR agenda are shown below.

The key components of corporate social responsibility

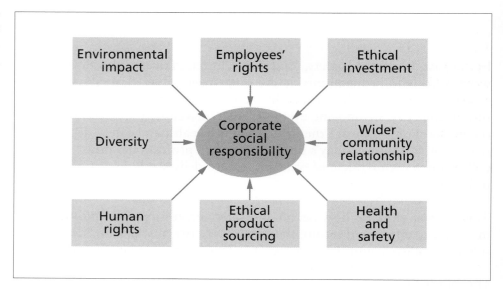

In the UK and other developed nations, there's legislation to cover most of these components. Sadly, in developing and emerging economies, such provisions are not always present.

Forward-thinking organisations aren't content with just putting a tick in the box that says "We comply with the relevant legislation." They influence their supply chain to do the same, as well as looking for the next piece of best practice to improve their performance.

It's important to demonstrate that your organisation is 'ethical' because this is increasingly what the public and investors expect. In the previous chapter, we discussed the power of the media. With this in mind, it's clear that embracing CSR is not only the right thing to do for the people in your organisation; it will also help give you a competitive advantage – it will make your organisation stand out from the crowd.

Synergies
There are many similarities between health and safety and the other areas that make up the CSR agenda. Arguably, those synergies are strongest in environmental management, employees' rights and diversity.

Environmental management
The link between health and safety and the environment is one that many individuals and organisations exploit. Given the similarities, this isn't surprising.

Legislation
There are clear examples of when the two topics combine to form 'meaty' legislation, such as the Control of Major Accident Hazard Regulations 1999 (COMAH). Among other things, COMAH requires adequate emergency planning. The health and safety aspect of this involves making sure people both on and off site are safe, while the environmental aspect considers the protection of the local and global environment.

Of course, there are some differences. Health and safety legislation tends to be based on a risk management approach, while environmental law centres on using best available options and target setting.[7] But don't be fooled: both areas have all-encompassing Acts. The Health and Safety at Work etc Act places a general duty on employers to provide a safe working environment, which arguably they've failed to do if there's an accident. Similarly, the Environmental Protection Act 1995 places a duty of care on employers,[8] which can be used as a basis of a prosecution even if the environmental incident falls outside the scope of any specific legislation.

Management systems
Health and safety and environmental management both rely heavily on management systems. As we'll see in Chapter 5, one management system is fairly similar to another. Some of the names may change but essentially their aim is always the same: to manage an issue in a structured and systematic way. In fact, they're so similar that options are also available to integrate environmental and health and safety management systems to make a 'one-stop shop'.

Tools – risk assessment
There are striking similarities between the environmental aspect and impact process and a health and safety risk assessment. The process of assessing an environmental aspect takes the work activity, project or product and asks what could happen as a result, while an environmental impact assessment looks at the effect an aspect will have on the environment. The end result is to focus on ways to mitigate any negative effects. Bringing risks and controls together in the form of a risk assessment is much the same thing, but considers what could cause harm to people as a result of work activities.

Tools – safe systems of work

Environmental operating procedures are similar to safe systems of work. Both explain how to do the job to prevent harm occurring, either to the environment or people.

Tools – incident reporting and investigation

Health and safety professionals find accident reporting and investigation vital as a way of measuring the success of the overall safety system and identifying areas for improvement. Environmental practitioners use reports and investigations of environmental incidents in a similar way.

Driving efficiencies

Good health and safety management not only reduces accidents but should also improve productivity and efficiency, and should therefore directly affect the bottom line. Likewise, and possibly with more tangible results, well-thought-out environmental programmes, such as segregating waste streams for recycling, using larger waste receptacles and having reduced collections, can become cost-neutral or even revenue generating.

Engagement

At the heart of all of this, though, is the need to get everyone in the organisation truly engaged. Whether it's getting directors' attention or encouraging employees to follow procedures, engagement is key to health, safety and environmental management. Similar tools and techniques are used in both disciplines.

Other topics

It may not be immediately obvious how the safety professional can influence or positively contribute to the rest of the CSR agenda. Traditionally, health and safety has stopped at the factory gates, dealing only with the way work is managed inside the workplace. There are opportunities to influence elsewhere, but to achieve this, safety professionals must break out of their silo.

Human rights, ethical product sourcing and investment

For an organisation's approach to CSR to mean anything, the suppliers it buys materials, products and services from must also be working towards similar CSR objectives. If they're not, it undermines what your organisation is trying to achieve.

Many organisations ask for information on their suppliers' health and safety performance and arrangements, but are they asking the right questions and does anyone ever check the answers? There's a real opportunity for the health and safety professional to add value to this process, not only by making sure that sensible information is requested (for example, information that can be interpreted across national boundaries), but also by making sure it's interpreted in the right way and is independently verified. This is a logical extension to the arrangements organisations already use to vet contractors who do work for them.

The same can be applied to investments. Indeed, it can often be relatively easy both for you and anyone checking your organisation's ethical credentials to find out the CSR performance of companies you invest in. For example, would you want your organisation's pension fund invested in a business that was killing or seriously injuring people because it didn't have suitable safety arrangements in place?

Supporting the wider community

An organisation's health and safety function can help achieve CSR goals by supporting the wider community through sponsorship and awareness-raising. If used in the correct way, these activities can help to achieve the broader strategic aims of the safety profession.

There are lots of sponsorship opportunities available. Many safety initiatives go beyond workplace safety by taking in road and home safety. Some examples are shown in the table on the next page.

Conclusion

The world of work is changing and health and safety is being incorporated into the bigger issue of CSR. This is no bad thing, as it enables health and safety to be raised even further up the corporate agenda.

The safety professional should not shy away from or resent the 'interference' of CSR as it provides significant opportunities for health and safety to achieve greater prominence. As part of a wider CSR programme, the contribution of good health and safety to the organisation's competitive edge becomes clearer. As we discussed in Chapter 1, the management principles that support good health and safety performance can be transferred to other disciplines. The links to other functions of the organisation provided by CSR allow health and safety professionals to spread their message further than if they remained in their safety silo.

Examples of supporting the wider community through health and safety-related programmes

Opportunity	Benefits	Cost
Sponsorship of a 'safety event', eg a safety award in a customer's or supplier's sector	• Powerful advertising direct to the target market • Competitive advantage (brand associated with taking safety seriously) • Opportunity for a deal with the event organisers to have key people mixing with attendees	Likely to be significantly less than a targeted marketing campaign
Sponsorship of a student, eg for NEBOSH qualification, an undergraduate placement, MSc, PhD	• Identification and development of new talent for the organisation • The student gains valuable real-life experience while the organisation gets an extra pair of hands • Research projects are cheaper than if undertaken independently and can be tailored to the needs of the organisation	• NEBOSH: cost of course • Undergraduate placement: around £15,000 for 12 months • MSc: £6,000 upwards • PhD: negotiated contribution towards fees
Donation to a safety-related charity	• Good advertising opportunities • Can be offset against tax • Supports wider health and safety strategies through the charity's campaigns and lobbying	Open-ended – most charities will be glad to accept any contributions
Delivering awareness training in schools and colleges	• Raises awareness of the organisation's brand among future employees and customers • Supports the wider aims of improving risk awareness and accident reduction	Minimal
Giving health and safety support to local community groups	• Advertising opportunity – eg 'Scout camp goes ahead thanks to Company X'	Minimal

Chapter 3: The world-class health and safety professional

It's common for health and safety team structures to be hierarchical and for one person to do everything in the area they're responsible for. Unfortunately, this can pose a number of challenges for their manager and the organisation, including:

- over-reliance on one person – what happens, for example, when that person is on holiday?
- an unmanageable workload for the safety professional
- a lack of capacity in the safety professional's workload to allow them to do 'value-added' safety work.

As a profession we're unlikely to be in a situation where we have too many safety professionals in an organisation, particularly during poor economic conditions. It's therefore important for us to think differently about how we work and what services we provide. This chapter discusses a number of ways to overcome some of these challenges in order to provide the foundations on which to build a world-class health and safety service, both in relation to what we do and how we present ourselves.

A world-class health and safety professional: the role

If the 'clipboard and cagoule' approach is one that the profession needs to get away from, the obvious question is "What do world-class health and safety professionals look like?" It's important to realise that the role they perform is quite different from the traditional approach – it's probably only about 20 per cent 'traditional' technical health and safety and 80 per cent general management skills, as shown in the diagram on the next page.

Traditionally, health and safety has been the job that you get given when the organisation wants you 'out of the way' or you're winding down to retirement. Now, though, it's used as a stepping stone to more senior management positions, as it's recognised that being a world-class health and safety professional is about good management – and every organisation needs that.

The role is not about banging your fist on the table and demanding that people do things. Rather, it's about providing:

The make-up of
the modern safety
professional's job

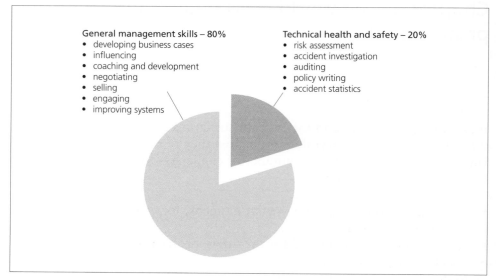

General management skills – 80%
- developing business cases
- influencing
- coaching and development
- negotiating
- selling
- engaging
- improving systems

Technical health and safety – 20%
- risk assessment
- accident investigation
- auditing
- policy writing
- accident statistics

- accurate information about safety issues facing the organisation and their likely impact on safety and financial performance
- a range of workable and cost-effective solutions (with a preferred option) to these issues.

The principle is that the organisation's bosses can use your information to make informed business decisions about how the organisation is going to manage its risks. In other words, the safety professional provides the advice and guidance but ultimately the decision is taken in a broader business context.

A world-class health and safety professional: the person
It almost goes without saying that all safety professionals need a minimum level of supporting knowledge – this is recognised by IOSH in its different categories of membership. The National Examination Board in Occupational Safety and Health's (NEBOSH) National General Certificate and National Diploma provide the most common route to gaining the necessary knowledge base, but there are increasing numbers of people entering the profession from the under- and postgraduate routes. If more health and safety professionals pass the NEBOSH National Diploma and other higher courses, the educational standards of the profession as a whole will increase. These educational standards should be a mandatory requirement, an issue on which IOSH has been lobbying the government for some time.

But being an effective health and safety professional is about a lot more than just qualifications. Your approach to your job is critical. Many safety professionals seem to develop a number of bad habits. Some are presented below, along with ways to avoid them.

A thousand words

Often, in their desire to get their message across, safety professionals tend to use a thousand words when 10 or 20 will do. It's important to remember to be concise – it will endear you more to your audience. If they want more information, you can always provide it on request.

Presentations

If you're unsure about how to deliver an effective presentation, find out who your organisation's best salesperson is and then go and watch them delivering a 'pitch' to a potential customer. They'll almost certainly stand up, speak with passion, be amusing and confident, and probably not use any notes.

- **Stand up:** This is important! It creates a natural focal point for the audience and allows you to have eye contact with them. It says: "I'm here and I'm confident about what I'm talking about, so listen up."
- **Passion:** Speaking with passion and conviction is vital. If you come across as bored or speak in a monotonous voice, how can you expect your audience to be excited and interested in what you're saying?
- **Telling a joke:** It's true that some people can't tell jokes – if you're one of them, don't try. But if you can, don't be afraid to bring a little humour into your presentation. It will help break the ice and endear you to the audience – remember, health and safety does not have to be boring.
- **Be confident:** The chances are, unless you're talking to a room full of other safety professionals, you'll know more about the subject than your audience, so be confident.
- **Holding notes:** You don't need to hold your notes. If you're using a slide presentation, the idea is that the slides have a small amount of text on them and act as a prompt for you to talk around. In other words, have an idea about what you want to say and say it – it will be far more powerful and natural. By all means have key points to hand in case you get a detailed question, but only refer to them when necessary.

Pick your fights

Try not to fall into the trap of arguing with everything. Some fights you're just not going to win. But don't ignore them either – highlight the problem in writing and chip away at it. On the other hand, there'll be some issues that you'll have to be passionate about and refuse to let go, particularly if someone is likely to be seriously injured. Wherever possible, try to get out of your silo and think of the bigger picture – some issues will resolve themselves without you falling on your sword for them.

Solutions

The generic solutions safety professionals come up with generally work in about 85 per cent of situations. It's OK to use a tried and tested method if it works. The remaining 15 per cent of situations demand more of your 'value-added' time so that you can develop more bespoke solutions to meet particular requirements.

Expand your horizons

In Chapter 2, we explored the idea that health and safety is a subject that overlaps into lots of other areas in an organisation. This means that there are many opportunities to expand existing skills and knowledge and acquire new ones. Not only does this make your life more interesting, but it also makes you more valuable to your organisation and the safety profession as a whole.

Arranging health and safety differently to create capacity

Individuals or teams who work in a silo are too focused on their specific job and fail to acknowledge or take into account the wider organisational perspective. One way round the silo approach is to adjust the roles and responsibilities of the safety team so that you can free up more time for value-added work with the same number of staff. After all, it's this work that will really change the organisation's safety performance and culture.

The central feature is to divert the more trivial aspects of the job away from the safety professionals to a central co-ordinator who's at the end of a phone or email inbox. The ideal candidate for this role would be someone in the team's administrative support (following some formal lower-level safety training). To help build the case for this, you may find it useful to talk to the team to find out the subjects of most of their telephone calls and emails. You'll probably find that they're often from managers asking for copies of documents and the like. If you refer them to the co-ordinator they'll probably get what they want a lot faster, too – the co-ordinator is available to help at the time of the request, while the senior safety professional may be busy elsewhere or even off site.

Some of the contacts may be questions starting "How do I do…?" or "How should I deal with…?" In these cases the co-ordinator can either help over the phone or arrange for the most appropriate member of the frontline safety team to visit the manager in person.

In effect, this approach filters a large proportion – it may be as high as 90 per cent – of all contacts that would otherwise go straight to the safety team and distract them from other things. From experience, this approach can increase job satisfaction at all levels of the team and it also helps you to develop a 'knowledge bank' of questions or problems and their answers or solutions that matches your organisation's needs.

Managing the customer relationship

We've seen that the role of a world-class safety professional is more about developing and using general management skills than using technical safety skills. This is especially true of managing your relationship with your 'customers'. The word 'customer' can refer to anyone you provide a service to, whether within your organisation or outside. Essentially, managing the customer relationship comes down to three key things:

- understanding your customers and their needs
- making sure you can supply the products and services that your customers need
- being able to deliver the products and services professionally, punctually and cost-effectively.

In later chapters we'll discuss how to work out your customers' needs and how to develop products and services that are 'fit for purpose'. Once you've done that, what then? How do you make sure you can deliver what they want, when they want it? Typically, you've got three choices:

- increase the head count of the safety team
- change your ways of working to free up some capacity for the team
- develop service level agreements (SLAs).

The first option is unlikely to happen – at least not immediately. The answer is often a mixture of freeing up capacity and developing SLAs. Of course, if the SLAs don't meet your customers' requirements, you may be able to get them to support your case for more staff or resources. Their contribution may carry more weight than your voice alone.

In a nutshell, SLAs define what you'll do and when. Typical health and safety-related agreements include:

- All lost time accidents will be investigated by the safety professional. The investigation will start within one working day of the incident being reported.
- Where five or more working days' advance notice is given of a visit by an enforcing authority, a safety professional will attend the visit to support the local manager.

Before starting to negotiate with your customers about the timings to be included in the SLAs, you need to work out the likely demand on your time. Without this information, you could be setting yourself up to fail. The worked example opposite shows a simple way of determining whether you can meet their demands.

This is only an estimate of the safety professional's 'supply and demand' based on their previous experience. But it does show that there is some scope for them to deliver value-added projects in the 73 'free' days.

Developing SLAs and working out the supply and demand allows the safety professional to quantify the work they do. There is an added advantage to setting SLAs as they provide measures of how they're performing beyond the organisation's basic measure of safety performance.

Conclusion

If you want to meet the needs of organisations in the 21st century, it's important to expand your role beyond that of the traditional technical specialist towards being a good manager. There are some common things that safety professionals do that hold them back from becoming world class, and yet they tend to be easy to resolve once they're identified and have been accepted by the individual.

There are opportunities to change the way you think and do things to create more time for you to go and provide support and help where it's needed the most. One way is to set SLAs, as these not only help to demonstrate where extra resources are needed and when, but they also help the organisation to decide which risks they want to manage and in what way, having heard your advice. In the end, health and safety is just another business decision. In the next few chapters, we'll look at more ways to free up time by working smarter.

Work plan forecast – demand			
Product or service	Quantity	Delivery time per unit (days)	Total delivery time (days)
Lost-time accident investigation	12	1.5	18
Enforcing authority visit support	8	2	16
Site audits	40	1.5	60
Managers' training	16	1.5	24
Safety committee support	4	1	4
Managers' meetings	16	1	16
Insurance claims support	6	1	6
Total demand			**144**

Work plan forecast – supply	
Planned commitments	**Days**
Annual workable days	260
Holiday entitlement	25
Bank holidays	8
Estimated sickness	5
Continuing professional development	5
Total days already committed	43
Total available days	**217**

Work plan forecast – summary	
Demand	144 days
Supply	217 days
Difference	73 free days available

Worked example of a supply and demand forecast

Chapter 4: The health and safety strategy

People can often get bogged down in the small details. To avoid this, every function in your organisation should have a clearly defined strategy linked to the organisation's overall aims.

Getting this 'bird's eye view' is sometimes difficult – sometimes there isn't time, and sometimes we don't have the tools we need. This chapter presents several ways to help overcome these shortcomings and develop a sound health and safety strategy.

What is a strategy?
Simply put, a strategy is a plan to help realise longer-term goals – developing it doesn't have to be a difficult exercise! The process is shown schematically below.

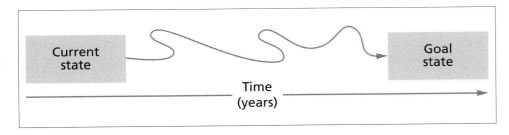

A simplified representation of strategy development

Goal state
It's often easiest to start by defining what your goals are. Health and safety goals are likely to include:

- developing a positive and mature safety culture
- reducing accidents, cases of work-related ill health and incidents
- changing behaviours towards safe working.

These are easily linked to the wider organisational goals of improving employee engagement, being an employer of choice and driving efficiencies.

Current state
Having worked out where you want to be, you need to work out where you are now. There are several ways of doing this. Commissioning an

external audit of the organisation's health and safety arrangements and culture is a common choice for safety professionals, but it has drawbacks. For example, you'll just be seen as the messenger, it can be a bit of a 'cop out' and, of course, audits are usually expensive.

If an external audit is not appealing, then it can be done internally – Chapter 7 discusses how to put together an internal audit. It can also be useful to run a series of 'focus groups' to get people from various parts of the organisation to give their views. But a word of caution: running focus groups isn't something you can just launch into. You need to be clear on what you hope to get out of the process and the members of the group will need to be confident that what they say won't be used against them. You'll also need a strong facilitator who is independent enough to prevent bias and increase the group's confidence – this person may well be external to the organisation.

Most of the time, though, you'll have a good idea of where you are at the moment and what you need to do to improve. This can be expressed in the form of a well-known management tool called a SWOT analysis.

Health and safety SWOT analysis
SWOT analyses are commonplace in modern organisations. They identify strengths, weaknesses, opportunities and threats.

- **Strengths** are the things the organisation does well in relation to health and safety – they help you achieve the goal state.
- **Weaknesses** are the areas that aren't yet supporting your drive towards the goal state. If you know what your weaknesses are, you can work out which processes, procedures or policies need tweaking to gain maximum impact. Identifying weaknesses can often give you some 'quick wins' – things that can be easily changed and will make a big difference.
- **Opportunities** are features that the organisation is not currently exploiting but needs to embrace to achieve the goal state.
- **Threats** are aspects that may prevent you achieving the goal state or make it more difficult. They may consist of activities that aren't being done but should be, bad practices that need to be changed, or areas that need improvement – legal compliance is a common example.

The gap
Irrespective of how you identify the current state, the key is to determine the course of action to help achieve the goal state. You need to address the areas your SWOT analysis identified as weaknesses, opportunities and threats.

Strategies tend to be designed to operate over the medium and long term, so it often helps to break the work down into a work plan for the coming years. If, for example, you identify middle management engagement as a particular weakness, you may decide to take the course of action shown below.

Strategic element	Year	Action
Engagement	1	• All middle managers will attend a one-day formal health and safety training course • A safety professional will attend all managers' team meetings to give safety messages a higher priority
	2	• Run a project to determine the cost of accidents to the organisation, championed by the finance director • Work with HR to implement a safety-related objective that can be included in a performance-related bonus
	3	• Set up middle manager safety focus groups

Possible actions to improve weak middle management engagement

It's important not only to record what actions you intend to take and when, as well as the change you expect to see, but also to show where this fits into the overall strategy. While the actions in the table above may not seem like a lot, remember that there'll be other areas that need addressing at the same time, all of which will require your time to set up, deliver and maintain. As you devise your plan, it's worth linking the elements together to make sure that they happen in the right order. If you need X to happen before you can do Y, then plan for X to be implemented before you plan to do Y.

Programme planning

It can be useful to use a simple tool to help plan your programme's priorities. You should use this alongside the supply and demand forecast model discussed in the previous chapter, as this shows how much time you have to deliver the programmes. The aim is to prioritise your work. An example of a high priority project is achieving legal compliance in an area which currently poses a threat to the organisation.

Some prioritising tools are rather complicated, but they needn't be. The diagram overleaf shows a simple example with a structured methodology, which is used by many organisations. It's based on two measures:

A commonly used programme prioritisation tool

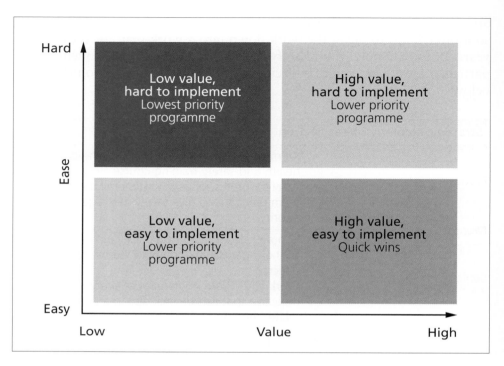

- ease of implementation in terms of time, cost and effort
- the value of the programme in terms of its contribution to achieving the goal state.

You also need to consider your organisation's appetite for a particular programme. If the organisation isn't ready for your idea yet, why spend all that time, money and effort on it when it could be used more effectively elsewhere? It's vital to identify the areas where you'll get the 'biggest bang for your buck'.

Risk profiling

Health and safety strategies often prioritise improvements to skills in poorly performing areas of the organisation, but you must first identify the poor performers. You can do this with a simple risk profiling tool – this approach works particularly well in multisite organisations. It allows each site to be compared with all the others. It can also be clearly linked to the coaching and development audit discussed in Chapter 7, as it enables you to identify which sites most need your help.

The tool is based on a blend of objective and subjective measures that create a rating which can be aligned to a risk level: high, medium or low.

Measure	Scoring
Number of RIDDOR-reportable accidents	Actual number
Number of employers' liability insurance claims	Actual number
Number of Improvement Notices	1 Improvement Notice = 10 points
Number of Prohibition Notices	1 Prohibition Notice = 25 points
Previous audit score	100 minus the previous score, so a previous score of 82% = 18 points

Common objective measures used in risk profiling tools

Measure	Scoring
Senior manager's score	Out of 100, given by the manager based on his or her view of how well the site is managed in general (100 is bad, 0 is perfect)
Safety professional's score	Out of 100, given by the safety professional based on his or her view of how well the site manages safety (100 is bad, 0 is perfect)

Common subjective measures used in risk profiling tools

The tables above show some typical objective and subjective measures used in risk profiling tools.

The strength of this approach is that it allows each organisation to use the same tool irrespective of how good or bad its safety performance is. This is because the risk ratings can be set by each organisation to reflect its performance. There are, of course, other performance measures that can be used, such as headcount, employee turnover and site profitability – but be careful not to fall into the trap of over-analysing.

It's broadly accepted that safety is a barometer of how well a site is managed. If all the business key performance indicators are positive, then most of the time safety will be well managed too. The senior manager responsible for the site should have a good handle on this – this is why their scoring is a very important measure. Remember that the senior manager whose opinion you canvass should not be the site manager – they're likely to give a biased view.

The critical thing to remember about this tool is that it points you in the right direction. The chances are it won't be completely accurate and it must be seen as dynamic and evolving, so that you can update things as you go along. A worked example is shown below.

		Site name								
		A	B	C	D	E	F	G	H	I
Number in last two years	RIDDORs	4	0	2	6	0	0	0	3	4
	Claims	5	2	3	4	1	0	1	2	2
	Improvement Notices	0	0	0	10	0	0	0	0	0
	Prohibition Notices	0	0	0	0	0	0	0	0	0
Previous audit score		9	6	9	15	6	4	1	7	7
Senior manager's score		55	45	50	70	25	25	25	50	65
Safety professional's score		55	40	50	80	20	20	10	55	80
Total		128	93	114	185	52	49	37	117	158
Risk rating		High	Mid	Mid	High	Low	Low	Low	Mid	High

A worked example of a risk profiling tool output

Conclusion

It's sound management practice to have a plan of where you're going. Forming a health and safety strategy is therefore not just best practice to give the safety professional a line of sight – it's expected by organisations and their stakeholders.

Developing a robust safety strategy doesn't require a great deal of work but delivering it can be onerous. The tools, ways of working and programmes presented in this book will help you lighten some of that load, while the programme prioritising tool and the risk profiler discussed in this chapter will help you to put your tasks in order and identify where you can get the time to deliver them.

Chapter 5: Health and safety management systems

To manage health and safety effectively, you need a robust management system. The law, especially the Management of Health and Safety at Work Regulations 1999, defines the need to manage health and safety.

In the UK there are two main approaches to occupational safety and health management systems (OSHMS):

- those that follow the model defined in the HSE's publication *Successful health and safety management*,[9] often referred to by its publication code 'HSG65'
- that described in the Occupational Health and Safety Assessment Series (BS OHSAS 18001:2007).[10]

When choosing or designing an OSHMS, it's important to remember the end aim. Too often, this is simply that a management system should be in place. This is only half the story, as the real aim is to have a system in place *and in use*.

Management systems can easily fall down because they become over-complicated and impractical, and because the 'engagement' piece of the jigsaw is often forgotten – in other words, the bit about getting people to follow it. This chapter explores how to avoid some of these pitfalls.

HSG65 or BS OHSAS 18001?

The intention of a management system is to define how a given process should be controlled. The two common types of OSHMS are shown schematically on the next page. Although each model is presented differently, they have many similarities, as the table on page 39 shows.

The approach in BS OHSAS 18001 has an advantage over HSG65 in that it's more widely recognised internationally and is similar to the ISO 9001 and 14001 standards for quality and environmental management. The OHSAS approach can therefore be helpful for organisations with multinational sites or trading partners. Also, to gain accreditation to BS OHSAS 18001, the complete system (paperwork and implementation) needs to be independently tested by an external body.

The HSG65
OSHMS model

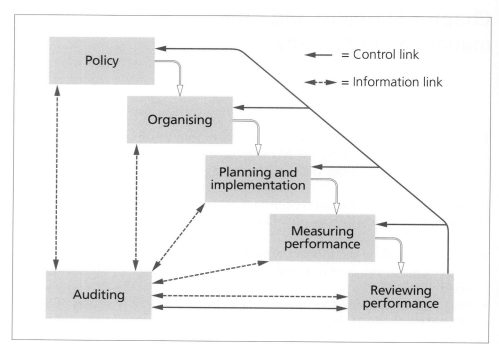

The BS OHSAS
18001 OSHMS
model

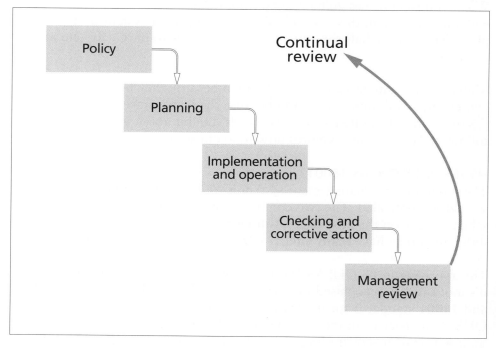

HSG65	BS OHSAS 18001	Element aim
• Policy • Organisation	• Occupational health and safety policy planning	Define organisational stance with clear roles and responsibilities
• Planning and implementation	• Implementation and operation	Implement the system
• Measuring performance	• Checking	Work out how effective the system is
• Reviewing performance and audit	• Corrective action • Management review • Continuous improvement	Regularly review performance at a strategic level and take steps to improve performance

Similarities between HSG65 and BS OHSAS 18001

This 'stamp of approval' can inspire greater confidence in the systems used to manage health and safety, but maintaining the accreditation is not always easy, particularly if people aren't engaged with it.

The cost and effort needed to achieve the BS OHSAS 18001 standard is relatively high when compared to HSG65. HSG65 is, therefore, perhaps more suited to small and medium-sized enterprises (SMEs). But even many of these take the view that if they've gone to the trouble of designing and implementing a good OSHMS, they may as well get it officially recognised through accreditation.

Writing a management system
It's common to find management systems in use that have been written by an organisation's safety professional in isolation, or at best with a few comments from someone else. This isn't the best way to implement an OSHMS, as it doesn't encourage ownership of the system among the people who are supposed to make it work.

For similar reasons, taking an OSHMS template from the internet or another 'off-the-peg' source and inserting your organisation's name is not necessarily appropriate either. You need to be sure that the source is trustworthy, the information the OSHMS contains is reliable and that it's applicable to your circumstances.

A best practice approach for developing a good bespoke OSHMS is to involve all functions and people who are affected. This also applies to those organisations that just need to formalise their existing informal arrangements, as it will provide an opportunity to re-evaluate what they already do. The table below lists a sample of OSHMS topic areas and likely interested parties.

A sample of OSHMS topic areas and likely interested parties

OSHMS topic	Interested parties
Hand–arm vibration	• Procurement • Occupational health • Human resources
Fire safety	• Property and facilities managers • Training • Fire alarm and emergency lighting service provider • Fire extinguisher service provider
Asbestos	• Property and facilities managers • Asbestos survey service provider

It goes without saying that you should include employee representatives as well as a selection of operational management and frontline employees in the discussions.

The safety professional's role in the group is to encourage debate about the relevant points and allow the discussion to develop until a solution that suits all parties is reached. Sometimes the safety professional may have to intervene, but from experience this is likely to be the exception rather than the rule. After all, 90 per cent of what people want to do will probably be acceptable from a health and safety point of view – it's only the remaining 10 per cent which may need the direct involvement of the safety professional.

You don't have to have everyone involved in developing the OSHMS present at every planning meeting – you can bring people with specialist knowledge in for particular discussions.

Critics of this inclusive approach argue that the meetings take up too much time and the OSHMS takes longer to write. But part of the safety professional's role is to keep the meeting on track. Discussing any potential issues at an early stage also allows problems to be identified and resolved at the time rather than delaying the process later on.

To give a structure to the working group meeting, you need to have done some preparation to help direct the group discussion. The easiest way to do this is to 'brainstorm' the issue concerned. After an initial brainstorming session, you can expand on it by cross-referencing the points to relevant legislation or guidance and making notes of any gaps. The diagrams below show typical brainstorming outputs for a defect reporting system and using computers.

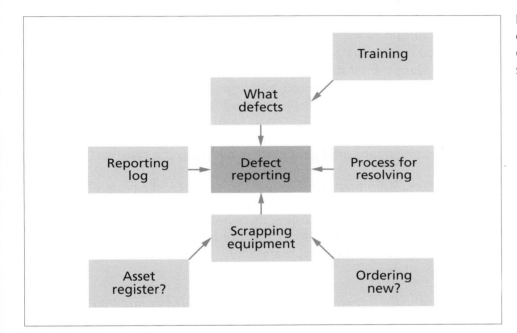

Brainstorming output for a defect reporting system

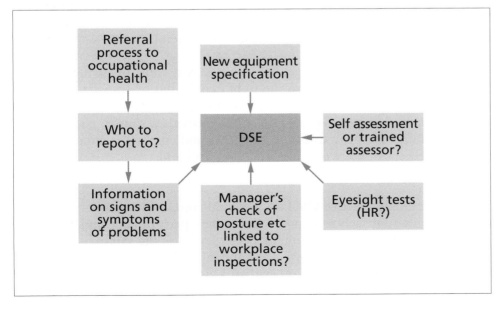

Brainstorming output for an OSHMS for computer use

From these exercises and the discussions that follow, the detail can be created and recorded in the normal fashion using the relevant management model. When completing this, the OSHMS is generally written in clinical language and uses a rigid hierarchy of titles and lower-level headings.

Getting engagement

A common output of the process to create an OSHMS is a long document that is issued to all work locations with an instruction to the manager that they are to read it, brief their teams and implement it. Although some organisations provide the manager with training to do this, generally this approach usually only succeeds in demotivating people. For example, if a local manager can only order new tools from an approved list supplied by head office, why does he or she need to know the authorisation process for procuring new tools and getting them added to the approved list?

You need to consider how people are going to access the parts of the OSHMS that are relevant to them. As we've seen, many organisations use the 'scatter-gun' approach of issuing the whole thing to everyone every time it's updated. The cost of doing this can be significant and arguably the money could be better spent, particularly if people are not going to use the OSHMS anyway.

One solution to the problem is to upload the OSHMS onto your intranet or distribute CD-ROMs to each department so that staff can refer to it when they need to. But even this only means that people can refer to the technical detail when they're not sure of something – it does not mean that they'll follow the management system in general.

To help overcome this challenge, you can add real value by giving the relevant parts of the OSHMS to the right people and by translating the technical speak into work instructions or flow charts. Some examples of these are shown on pages 43 and 44. These provide a simple, quick reference source for busy frontline managers and employees alike. These can then be kept in the work area and close to hand.

Conclusion

A clearly defined, effective OSHMS is a vital component in any organisation's approach to improving its safety performance and culture. But designing them has traditionally been viewed as the safety professional's 'bread and butter', and something done in isolation with little thought of the end result other than a tick in the box.

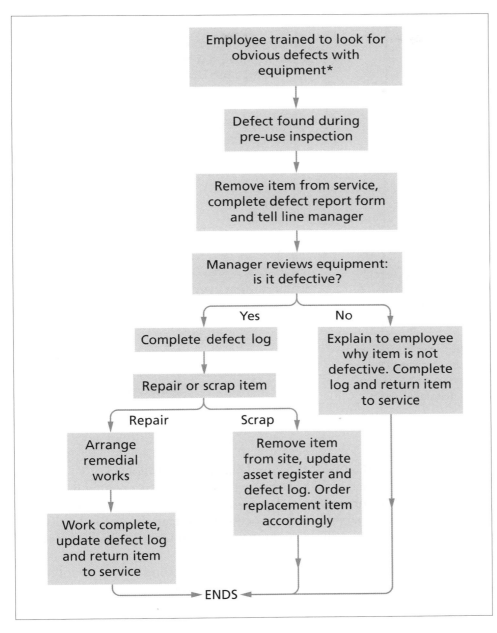

A defect reporting reference guide for front line managers and employees

* Obvious defects include:
* electrical cables: bare wires, nicks in cabling
* hydraulic equipment: oil leaks
* general machinery: start and stop (including emergency stop) controls not working; broken or defeated interlocks; missing guards

A reference guide
to computer use
assessment for
front line
managers and
employees

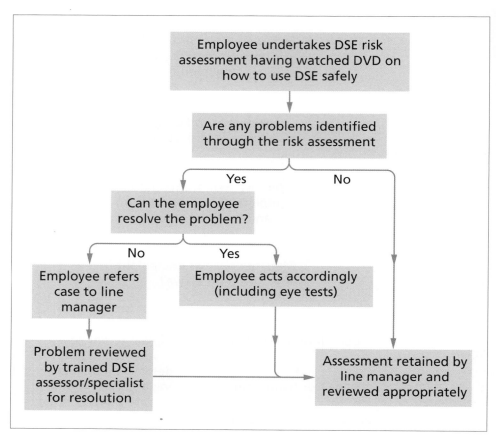

To make sure that the OSHMS is implemented and followed, it's important to get a real-world perspective, which means opening it up to input from a wider organisational audience. This will help improve engagement and ownership of the process, but it can also help identify possible inefficiencies in the way the organisation manages its business.

Developing an OSHMS is only part of the job. Getting people to follow it is vital and this is probably the hardest thing to do. But without everyone's support, you'll just be measuring how unsuccessful the OSHMS is.

An OSHMS should be simple to use and easy to follow, and its contents should be acceptable to all – there's something wrong if health and safety gets in the way of doing the job.

Chapter 6: Health and safety training programmes

Training is fundamental: it's the way employees learn about how they should do the job and develop new skills and knowledge. This is as true of health and safety as it is of any other aspect of a job, and it starts on day one. Often, the first introduction a new employee has to their organisation's views on health and safety is through its induction programme. Ongoing training is also a crucial element to working and managing safely.

Despite the best intentions, mistakes are often made when designing and delivering health and safety training. Common errors in delivering training include putting too much emphasis on legal requirements, using too many slides and/or too much text on each, and going into far too much detail. You only get one chance to make a good impression, so you must get it right first time.

Many organisations aim to avoid these common pitfalls by outsourcing health and safety training to an experienced, competent training provider. In this case, you need to know how to pick the right provider for your organisation from the many hundreds of companies who advertise in the trade press, appear on internet searches and send you unsolicited mail.

But using an external provider isn't right for everyone, and this chapter outlines simple ways to develop effective health and safety training courses in house, as well as discussing the key aspects of finding external training providers.

Designing health and safety training programmes

Regardless of the subject of your training, you should follow a basic development process, shown at the top of the next page. In many organisations, though, training courses are simply written and then delivered by the safety professional, with no way of knowing whether they've had any effect.

In the modern workplace, safety training should be more than just a course. It should be an ongoing process that considers more than traditional classroom learning and includes post-learning measurement.

The general process for delivering a health and safety training programme

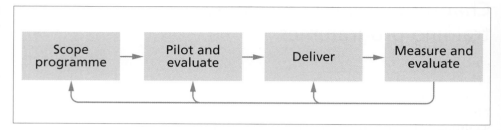

Planning the programme

Working out what the course is going to deliver and how is fundamental, and has to be linked to the training needs analysis that identified the gap in training in the first place. You should plan the course with input from representatives of several departments of the organisation, rather than trying to do it all by yourself. The next diagram shows the likely stakeholders and what each one contributes.

Likely stakeholders in a health and safety training programme and their contribution to its success

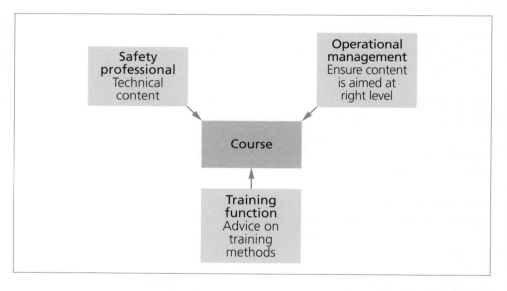

The key to success here is not to allow this exercise to become too big a job. The important outputs are:

- learning outcomes – at the end of the programme, what should the delegates be able to do?
- accurate course content that's pitched at the right level and helps achieve the learning outcomes
- varied training methods that are appropriate to the learners to enable their engagement.

When all this is in place, the programme can be delivered – but not before it's piloted. This is particularly important if the programme is to be delivered many times. Spending a little extra time in the preparation phase will pay dividends in the long run.

Pilot and evaluate

The pilot is about performing a trial of the programme and getting feedback from the delegates about how they felt it helped them to do their job more effectively. In doing this, you need to seek the opinions of the delegates, but this must be more than the normal 'happy sheets' that seem to be given out at the end of most training courses. It's widely accepted that these just measure how much the delegate liked the trainer and what they thought about the lunch! Being open with the delegates that it's a trial and asking for their feedback is the best option. Don't forget to gather any feedback they give to their manager after the course, too.

In an ideal world you would monitor the delegates' behaviour in the workplace to see if they've taken the training on board and acted in the way the programme set out for them to do. However, in the fast-paced world in which we find ourselves, this is unlikely to happen except with the largest of training programmes.

The programme-scoping group should reconvene to review the feedback and agree any adjustments needed to the programme.

Delivery

This is the easy bit: the product has been designed, tested and proved to work. The challenge with the delivery phase is to ensure consistency in how it's delivered. This is a particular issue if more than one trainer delivers the programme.

A simple way round this is to devise trainer notes and for the trainers to sit in on the first few sessions so that they understand how the course should be delivered. Further into the roll-out of the training, 'dip checks' and other monitoring methods can be used, and are like those discussed in Chapter 7 in relation to monitoring auditors' scores.

Sometimes the training won't be delivered by safety professionals – it may be given by a team of generalist trainers. In this case, the safety professional needs to be satisfied that the trainers are competent to deliver the course. Competence refers not only to how to deliver the training (which shouldn't be a problem, given their job role), but also to their technical safety knowledge.

Trainers can often make safety training come alive with anecdotes and real-life examples. Delegates also often ask questions that veer away from the main content – and they expect an answer. While saying "I don't know but I'll find out" is acceptable, it's important to avoid a situation where the trainer feels pressurised into giving an answer immediately that turns out to be wrong. This could clearly have implications for the trainer and the organisation.

The way to overcome these problems is to give the trainers themselves some form of safety training. What form this takes depends on the course content – a basic site safety induction won't need the same level of understanding as a more in-depth course for line managers.

Measurement and evaluation

Having delivered the course, it's important to measure how effective the programme has been. As we mentioned before, 'happy sheets' are generally of limited value, so what other methods can we use? Measurement should be split into two parts:

- **Supporting knowledge.** It's vital that delegates understand the supporting knowledge of the programme. This can be tested through a written or practical test or a combination of both. Written tests can be marked after the course, but marking them during the course, with people calling out the answers, does have some clear advantages. Mistakes can be corrected instantly and feedback can be given as to why the answer was wrong. The trainer can also spot trends in the answers, which can give instant feedback on their performance and the suitability of the course content.
- **Learning transfer.** Once the delegates have the supporting knowledge, it's important that they apply it in their workplace. This can be measured through monitoring their accident performance, work observation sessions and workplace audits.

When training is outsourced, the measurement element tends always to be completed, as organisations want to make sure that they get value for money. You should apply the same principle to in-house programmes, as this will help you demonstrate further how you're adding value to the business.

The data gained from the evaluation can be used to review the whole process to see what went well and what didn't, helping you to design and deliver future programmes.

Training programme hints
The following hints will help you develop effective safety programmes:

- Your training should be more than a one-off intervention. If you start off with a traditional classroom-based session, make sure you follow it up with practical coaching and support in the learner's workplace.
- Courses should be full of examples to bring the topics alive. This will paint pictures in the delegates' minds, helping them to remember the theory behind them when they return to their workplace.
- Be snappy. The 'classroom' elements should be fairly short – if it's an all-day session, split it up into modules with plenty of breaks between them. Try not to cram too much in: it's better to cover less but make sure your delegates remember it, than to include everything but risk delegates forgetting most of it.
- Don't focus too much on the law. For example, if you're training managers how to do a risk assessment, do they really need to know word for word what the legislation says about risk assessment? Or is it more important that they understand the practical points of carrying out an assessment and have the skills they'll need to put the findings into practice?
- Give the right amount of detail. You need only enough detail for your delegates to follow the themes of the training. If they come across situations that need an understanding of the technical detail, that's when they need to call in the safety professional to help support the local manager.

External training providers

The alternative to developing and running safety training programmes in house is to arrange for an external training provider to do it all for you.

Whether you decide to go down this route will depend on your organisation's circumstances – one rule doesn't fit all. Some organisations may consider the cost of outsourcing acceptable if it means that their safety professional can get on and do other things, thus 'killing two birds with one stone'. Others may think that there's more value in them putting their message across themselves.

If you're considering an external training provider, you should bear in mind a number of points:

- Can they deliver accredited courses? Often organisations outsource training because they want their employees to undertake accredited safety courses, such as those offered by IOSH and the Chartered

Institute of Environmental Health. (It's possible for individual organisations to become accredited training providers, but this isn't normally cost-effective unless the number of delegates involved is large.)

- Are they willing to change their standard 'off the shelf' product to suit your organisation's specific needs? 'Off the shelf' products are just that – they haven't been written specifically for your industry, never mind your organisation's systems and requirements. They can often be tailored to cover your organisation's weak points, but you need to ask – don't presume training providers will do this automatically.
- Decide what you want them to deliver and then contact them. Often you can build up a shortlist of likely providers from the information you get from the initial contact, such as their price and how sensible their proposal sounds.
- Once you've got a shortlist, meet each provider face to face to explore the programme more and work out what makes them better than the next provider. Follow up references from other organisations they've worked with and, if possible, ask to see their trainers in action and to look at their course content. The same rules apply as for an in-house course: trainers must be entertaining and knowledgeable and the content must be snappy and relevant.
- When you've decided which provider you want to use, negotiate the price. Typically the price you're told at the beginning is not the cost they'll do it for – they'll have a lower price that they can offer and still make a reasonable margin. If you don't ask, you don't get.
- Negotiate a contract with clearly defined service level agreements. This may sound over the top, but experience suggests that it's essential to protect both parties. If the course provider is a reputable company, they'll have a generic contract ready for signing. Don't be afraid to get it checked out by your organisation's legal team to make sure that your interests are protected.

Conclusion

Training is a fundamental requirement of health and safety but it needs to be handled well to be effective. There needs to be a shift away from the traditional view of training being a one-off event. The training course should be part of a much broader programme of learning, which makes sure the knowledge gained in the course is applied in the workplace.

Outsourcing training is an alternative, but although it's often seen as an easier option, there are as many pitfalls with using external providers as in-house trainers. If you're thinking of going down this route, you should follow simple service selection and negotiation processes to make sure you get what you want at a price your organisation is willing to pay.

Chapter 7: A model for auditing

In Chapter 5, we saw that audits are an important part of any management system. They play a particularly crucial role in allowing you to be confident that the business is doing what it says it is. Thus their roots lie deeper in corporate governance.

There's a growing industry providing health and safety auditing services. While off-the-peg audits are undoubtedly effective, most companies would probably prefer their own bespoke auditing programme.

'Being audited' generally provokes feelings of dread among operational staff. There are several common reasons for this: occasionally the results are used as 'another stick to beat them with'; they are perceived as taking up lots of time; and often they're thought to be more hassle than they're worth.

Despite these views, audits are here to stay. They can be used not just to provide the necessary assurances and highlight areas for improvement as required by good corporate governance, but also to increase stakeholder engagement, improve safety performance and develop the organisation's safety culture.

This chapter outlines how to design an audit programme and suggests an audit model that organisations can pick up and use quite quickly.

Audit components

All too often, people get confused between inspections and audits. The HSE has acknowledged this point,[9] explaining that organisations often assume they're the same thing.

In its simplest form, an audit is a technique used to test how robustly an issue is managed when compared to a given standard. That standard could be legal requirements, organisational policy or industry best practice. In other words, an audit measures your performance against defined criteria, provides feedback on how well you're doing, and helps you set your future direction.

The basics

Most audit programmes have three basic components:

- an audit protocol
- a selection of sampling techniques
- high validity and reliability.

Protocols

Audits are carried out according to a set protocol. Essentially, this outlines what and how you audit and is typically a set of questions. There are lots of off-the-shelf audit programmes available, and when these are used to their full potential they can be extremely impressive. When you're deciding whether to use one of these programmes, you should be aware of the advantages and disadvantages associated with them. Some examples of each are shown in the table below.

Some of the advantages and disadvantages of typical off-the-shelf audit programmes

Advantages	Disadvantages
• The question set, guidance to determine the level of compliance, and the actions required to put a deficiency right have already been prepared • Software audit programs tend to be linked to a database, allowing very quick analysis of the data • The audit programme provider will often offer ongoing technical and user support as well as continual development of the programme to take account of new developments • Customers often have greater confidence in audits to an independent standard (but this depends on how well known the programme is)	• Most programmes require an initial fee and then a fee per licence (for each user); updates and support can also be expensive • Software packages can often do a lot more than your organisation needs, so that you don't use significant sections of what you've paid for, with a reduction in the return on your investment • A limited ability to make the programme organisation-specific can make it less useful • Off-the-shelf audit programmes are generic and often aren't successful in industries with unusual or very specific requirements

Given the choice, most organisations would prefer bespoke audit programmes. Unfortunately, they're often put off by the perception that they take a lot of time, effort and money to create, or are worried that they don't have the ability in house to do a good job. Realistically, creating an audit programme isn't that difficult; all that's needed is an understanding of the topic being considered and a logical mind.

As an example, let us take a relatively simple example of auditing compliance with a legal requirement – the health and safety policy statement. The Health and Safety at Work etc Act 1974, section 2, part 3, states that:

> … it shall be the duty of every employer to prepare and as often as may be appropriate, revise a written statement of his general policy with respect to the health and safety at work of his employees and the organisation and arrangements, for the time being in force for carrying out that policy, and to bring that statement and any revision of it to the notice of all his employees.[11]

The question set to determine how well the organisation is complying with this requirement would generally include the following:

- Is there a health and safety policy statement signed by the managing director (or a similar person) within the last 12 months?
- Does the policy statement outline the organisation's general position on health and safety?
- Is it displayed in a prominent position on the organisation's premises?
- Have all staff read it and are they aware of its contents?
- Is this formally recorded, for example in their employee training log?

Obviously more complex issues may take more time to think about, but the basic concept is the same.

Sampling techniques

A good audit is more than just taking things at face value. It's all about getting formal evidence to qualify the answer. Typically, the general gist of conversation in an audit is along the lines of: "Thank you for telling me that. Now can you prove it?" Different sampling techniques are used to gain the data on which you make your decision about how the area being audited is performing – it depends on what you're looking at.

Interviews with managers and employees are commonly used and are helpful in getting the necessary information (anecdotal or otherwise). It's worth remembering to go into interviews prepared: the interviewee's time is precious and they may already have negative views about audits, which will be reinforced if you waste their time. You also need to think about who you're talking to. You're likely to need different approaches, depending on whether you're talking to the site manager in a formal, pre-booked meeting or having an informal chat with an employee.

Inspections are used to make physical checks and observe working practices. Avoid simply working off a checklist – this can make you blind to the real problem because it's not on the list. And remember that we're trying to get away from the checklist image of health and safety! That said, it's understandable to want to structure auditing work, and it can be useful to have a few notes about likely issues to look out for.

Another common method of gathering data for an audit is to collate general management information, such as:

- accident and incident records
- sickness absence records
- numbers of referrals to occupational health
- employer's liability insurance inspection reports
- findings of the enforcing authorities when they visit.

Validity and reliability

It doesn't matter how much work you put into the audit protocol and collecting data if the audit isn't valid. If your audit doesn't appear to test what it claims to test, or if its results are questionable, you won't win the support of operational managers.

A major factor in achieving good validity is developing the audit protocol correctly. Once developed, it should be tested at a number of locations to see whether the audit delivers the same results that were expected. Remember that, ideally, the auditor shouldn't be the person who says whether the site is good or bad – this way, potential bias in the design and testing process is removed.

Reliability involves making sure that the same results are achieved if the exercise is repeated. This tends to improve when there is a smaller number of auditors involved, but defining 'reliability' can be difficult, since audits are just snapshots in time. But you need to avoid extreme variation in people's marking. Having a well-defined audit protocol will control this to some extent, but you also need to control the auditors' individual differences in interpretation. For example, some people may be extremely harsh in their view and others too lenient.

You can smooth out inconsistencies of this kind by 'levelling'. There are two main ways to do this:

- **Physical levelling.** This is where all the auditors are asked to audit the same location at the same time, following which they discuss the results and come to a standardised interpretation. This interpretation is then applied to all future audits.

- **Desktop levelling.** This works in cases where compliance with each audit question or category is defined by a numerical score. The exercise involves determining the average score for each auditor against each of the questions or categories. If all the auditors are scoring within 5 per cent of the overall mean score, you can be confident that the auditors are being consistent in their interpretation of the question and the situation presented to them. Any significant deviation from this would suggest either that the auditors are not being consistent or that the locations vary significantly in terms of safety management.

There are clear pros and cons for each method. The physical levelling is really useful at the start of the audit process to help get the auditors 'onto the same page' as each other. The desktop option is less labour intensive to start off with but it may still be necessary to bring the group together to carry out a physical levelling session to understand the differences thrown up by desktop levelling and to agree a way forward.

Best practice suggests it would be sensible to start off with the physical levelling and then review the auditors at a predetermined interval (eg every month) using the desktop review. Further physical levelling sessions can then be added as necessary, but probably at least every six months.

Value-added audit programme

We've seen that in modern business auditing is a given and therefore resources will be committed to it. If auditing is carried out correctly, there should be a positive impact on safety culture. The diagram on the next page shows a best practice audit programme, versions of which are used by many organisations. The programme has a number of merits:

- it frees up significant amounts of time for the safety professional to provide support where it's needed most (the poor performing sites) and other value-added programmes
- it advances the safety culture at a quicker pace than traditional audits
- it still gets the job of auditing done.

We'll now consider each of the elements in this programme in turn.

Policy

This part of the audit considers the effectiveness of an organisation's policies at complying with a defined standard. It's typically carried out by a safety professional as often as required by the organisation's needs and the number of changes made to the policies, procedures, legislation and industry guidance.

A best practice
six-point audit
programme

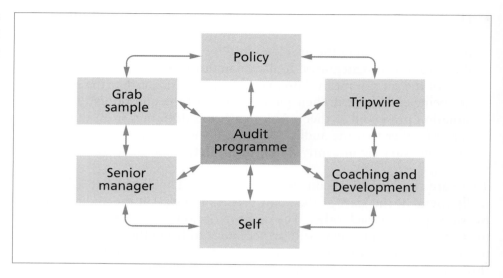

The findings help identify areas of the organisation's policies where weaknesses need to be dealt with, and they can be used to determine the organisation's health and safety strategy – see Chapter 4.

Tripwire

The tripwire collects data about individual site management of obvious high-risk health and safety issues, allowing them to be detected and corrected quickly. It's based on the assumption that most organisations have a compliance-type auditing function, which visits multiple locations to measure their compliance with organisational procedures on various issues linked to administration and financial management. There are clear parallels between this audit team's work and that of the safety auditor. If time and resources can be saved by exploiting these parallels, the safety professional can turn his or her attention to other things.

The tripwire simply builds on the existing compliance team audit by adding a number of health and safety-related questions. These are specific to the problems being experienced in the organisation, which is why they're linked to the policy audit above. In essence, the tripwire uses other people to be your eyes and ears.

Take, for example, a food retail shop, where one of the highest risks is of customers suffering slips, trips and falls on the same level. The protocol for the auditors to follow would be along the lines of that shown in the table opposite.

Audit statement: Slips, trips and falls on the same level are adequately controlled
Answer **yes** if all of the following statements are true, where applicable: • There are no spillages or other debris on the shop floor • Anti-slip mats are located at the entrance to the shop and at the fruit and vegetable aisle • Employees know what to do if there's a spillage • 'Wet floor' signs are available • There are no potholes or similar in the floor • Variations in floor level are highlighted • Display plinths aren't left with nothing on them • Stock isn't stored on the floor

The critical part of this audit is that you're keeping the obvious high-risk safety issues at the top of people's agenda – hence the name 'tripwire'. It's ideal to keep the protocol to around 10–15 key areas. For each possible deficiency noted, a standard set of corrections can be developed, making the life of the auditor easier.

It's also important to make sure that the auditors have the opportunity to highlight other hazards not covered in the audit. The organisation would be failing in its duty if it became blinkered and considered only what is included in the protocol. Naturally, the people carrying out the audit will need some training on what to look for. Most importantly, they'll need to know what to do if they're unsure about something: stop and ask the advice of a safety professional.

Coaching and development

If the tripwire creates capacity for you while maintaining the impetus of the audit, the coaching and development phase allows you to focus resources where they're needed most – the poor-performing locations.

But how do you know where your poor-performing sites are? You may have a gut feeling about some of them, but you may not know them very well, particularly if you have many to look after. It's therefore useful to develop a risk profiling tool that uses a blend of objective and subjective data to create a list of high, medium and low risk sites (see Chapter 4).

Once you've determined your organisation's risk profile, the hard work begins: supporting sites to improve their performance. The coaching and development audit will help you pinpoint the people, departments and knowledge areas that need most support. You can then offer site managers at the weaker locations coaching and support to enable them to understand what the problem is and how to implement systems or other control measures that raise their safety performance.

The way it works is simple: you walk round the site with the manager, helping them see the problems and explaining why they matter. This could be done via a standard modular presentation to ensure consistency of delivery. You can often start to solve some of the biggest issues with the manager immediately.

Ideally, if the manager solves the most important five or six problem areas with your support, he or she should then have had enough coaching and development to design and implement solutions to the less challenging ones themselves. This approach also ensures that the highest risks are dealt with directly by a safety professional.

The key to success with this is not to think that the work is finished when you leave the site. Feedback is integral to coaching and development, so plan to return to the site at a mutually convenient time, say in six weeks, to see how the manager is getting on.

This enables you to check that local managers are progressing along the right lines, offer more coaching and give feedback (both praise and suggestions for improvement). In the worst case, a follow-up visit will give you the evidence you need to take to their line manager to show that they just aren't doing what they should be. This makes safety a performance management issue – see Chapter 10.

Self

As the safety culture of the organisation develops, and when you feel it's time for operational managers to engage more with health and safety, you can introduce the self audit.

In the same way as for developing any audit, consider what areas you want the managers to look at and then develop a question set accordingly. In this case it could be linked to the common problem areas noted in the coaching and development audit. The self audit should not just look at paperwork; it should be a combination of observations of working practices and a paper-based management review.

Bear in mind that this kind of exercise can become a joke among managers, who regard it as a simple tick-box task. You should introduce it only when the safety culture has developed enough. Line managers who are committed to improving safety culture are more likely to take the self audit seriously, and a mature safety management system will have the necessary processes in place to check the validity of the audits.

You also need to remember that, as well as managing safety, managers have many other things to do and priorities to consider. It'll help them to accept your suggestions if you break down what you're asking them to do into manageable chunks. This won't just make it more likely that they'll do what you want – it also makes the whole process easier to administer.

The next thing to consider is the frequency of the self audit. Some organisations ask their managers to check two things a week, so that over the course of the year they complete 104 safety checks. Others ask managers to do 10 checks a month.

Don't forget that as the new process takes off, you'll get a lot of requests for your time to help put things right. An important factor in setting the self-audit frequency is your resource level – how many requests for help will you be able to handle each week or month, and will you be able to prioritise the most important issues effectively?

While this audit is aimed principally at engaging front-end managers, it can also be used to revitalise health and safety committee meetings, use the skills and experience of safety representatives more effectively, and develop team leaders' safety skills.

Senior management

This part of the programme is concerned with encouraging senior managers and directors to interact with frontline employees in a structured and systematic way about site health and safety practices.

The audit protocol at this level should be kept to four or five key questions that are clearly linked to the organisation's overall health and safety strategy, as this will help to show senior management commitment. The questions should not be detailed, complex or technical. Organisations that use this approach simply aim to demonstrate to frontline staff and managers that the senior management takes health and safety as seriously as other business concerns.

At the end of the exercise, the senior manager or director should talk the manager through what he or she has found, and the manager should agree a plan with the senior manager or director to put any shortcomings right.

Grab sample

This can be carried out by anybody after a small amount of training to explain to them what they're looking for. It can be used to give a quick snapshot of compliance with a specific issue at a large number of sites at the same time.

For example, as part of your organisation's occupational road risk programme, you may want to check that all drivers leaving your site are wearing their seatbelts. The people doing the checking could be from any part of the organisation, not just from the health and safety department, as long as they've been briefed about what to look for. They can then carry out the review simultaneously at a number of sites. Doing the samples simultaneously is critical, otherwise the first site visited could warn others to be 'on their guard', so the picture you'd get wouldn't reflect reality.

'Grab sampling' in this way also supports the development of a safety culture in areas of the organisation that don't traditionally think about safety a great deal, as it involves people from these areas directly in safety management. If staff who need to visit other parts of the organisation from time to time have taken part in a grab sampling exercise, they'll be more likely to understand and appreciate the safety rules they encounter.

We've discussed the main links between elements in the auditing model, but by now you should be able to see others that have not been explicitly noted. All the elements are interlinked and feed into the 'bigger picture', which provides the necessary assurance (or otherwise) that your organisation is doing what it said it would do.

Conclusion

Audits form a major and often a time-consuming part of the safety professional's job. They are a proactive safety management tool in the sense that they can highlight areas needing improvement before an accident happens, but like all tools they have shortcomings. They rely on the manager being audited to implement their recommendations and on the overall organisational structure to make sure the manager does this. In other words, audits won't work if you can't revisit the departments and sites you've audited to help them improve.

Chapter 8: Overcoming inaction

Engaging the unengaged is probably the hardest challenge safety professionals face and there's no one sure-fire way of succeeding. If there were, whoever thought of it would be very rich!

"How do you overcome inaction?" is a traditional question asked in job interviews for health and safety positions and the reality can be a source of much frustration for safety professionals the world over. This chapter suggests some ways of overcoming inaction at all levels of an organisation. They are mainly based on thinking about things differently and being more 'savvy'.

The traditional approach
As safety professionals we're taught that there are three reasons why health and safety should be taken seriously:

- legal obligations placed on employers and individuals
- moral considerations
- financial benefits in managing health and safety effectively.

While these are definitely good reasons why people should manage health and safety, they don't really go far enough if you're dealing with people who really don't want to do anything.

The legal argument
Laws are created to make people do something and are enforceable by various agencies and penalties. But that doesn't mean that people obey them.

Let's take as an example the use of hand-held mobile phones while driving. It's been illegal to do this in the UK for some time, yet how many people do you still see driving while holding a phone to their ear? The reasons they do it may be that they perceive the chances of being caught are low, or that even if they're caught, they feel that the penalties are too lenient to make them change their behaviour.

It'll come as no surprise that unscrupulous employers may be thinking along similar lines when it comes to health and safety in the workplace.

The moral argument

Nobody wants to be the one who has to knock on someone's door to explain that their loved one has had an accident at work and won't be coming home again. But, unless you've been in that unfortunate position yourself, it's very easy to forget because, thankfully, deaths at work are rare. The only sure way of getting this mindset to 'stick' would be a rise in the number of deaths – something we clearly don't want to happen.

Financial benefits

Justifying health and safety actions on financial grounds is a far better solution to the problem, but even then it's still very easy to be too simplistic about making the commercial argument. It's not usually a case of a simple statement such as 'Do this and you'll save on sick pay expense', for example.

To really get attention using this argument, you need to be commercially savvy in making sound business cases. They need to have positive forecasts not only for health and safety but for the wider business as well, to the extent that improved safety is almost the by-product of widening margins. But does it matter so long as the job gets done?

A different approach

In 1968 Dick Fosbury changed the high jump forever. He managed to jump higher than the other competitors in the Olympic Games of that year by using a different method of jumping. Instead of using the 'straddle jump' his contemporaries were using, he perfected a 'flop' that became known across the world as the 'Fosbury flop' – and it's still used today.

This example shows that thinking outside the box really does work. But while the theory works, putting it into practice is another matter, particularly when you've been brought up to believe that there's only one way to do something.

In overcoming inaction we need to turn things on their head. We should be asking why people won't do something rather than telling them why they should do it. Essentially, we need to remove their arguments for not doing something. In terms of health and safety, our approach needs to be based on three core elements:

- avoiding over-complication
- avoiding mentioning the law
- providing the material in bite-sized chunks.

Less experienced safety professionals often make the mistake of complicating everything, either by devising a convoluted safety system or by making people complete reams of paperwork. The message is clear: keep things simple. The more complicated things are, the less likely people are to do them.

It shouldn't be necessary to quote the law as a way of getting people to do what you want, as your plans should make ethical and business sense in their own right. If they don't, you probably need to find another way of explaining them. This is, after all, the fundamental spirit of the Health and Safety at Work etc Act.

Most people want to get health and safety right – nobody wants to be responsible for hurting someone else. So they'll try to do their best, but because they see it as a huge task, they chip away at one corner of it. Before long, they find they lack the skills and tools they need, they don't get very far and, demoralised, they give up. When we put it like that, who can blame them? Your job as a safety professional is to break the huge task down into bite-sized chunks that people can cope with more easily.

Understanding your audience

We noted in Chapter 6 that you wouldn't try to write a training course without first considering your audience. The same principle applies when trying to overcome inaction. Even in the most unengaged organisation, there'll always be some people who are interested in health and safety. The thing to do is to identify them along with the other key players.

You can do this by performing an 'engagement–influence' exercise (see the diagram on the next page). This is a common management model used to place key players appropriately on a graph in order to work out how well people have engaged with the subject.

The goal with this model is to have everybody, irrespective of their level of influence, showing high levels of engagement. Once you've placed everyone according to the model, it's important to use the results to help achieve your goal. For example:

High influence and high engagement, low influence and high engagement
People in these categories are where you want them to be. The key action with these people is to maintain their interest and momentum.

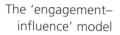

The 'engagement–
influence' model

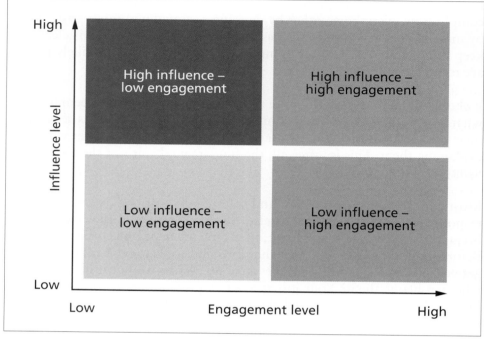

High influence and low engagement

These people are the ones with the real influence in the organisation and they're not switched on yet to what you're trying to do. You need to focus your attention on people in this group.

Low influence and low engagement

Although it's not ideal that this group of people isn't fully engaged with what you're doing, you obviously need to concentrate on those with more influence first.

Techniques

Having identified who you need to work on, it's important to start to understand the people individually by finding out about their personalities and motivations – as these will give clues as to how to approach them. Try to find some common ground, inside or outside work – this is a good ice breaker and helps people to warm to each other.

Peer pressure

In any group of people, the odds are that someone will already be on side. Once you've worked out who they are, you should work with them to develop their interest and help them prove to the rest of the group that what you're saying works and makes sense. It's often more effective to get someone inside the group to shout about how good something is than to get an outsider to give the message.

Language

In Chapter 1 we discussed the health and safety profession's 'clipboard and cagoule' image problem. It's important to break this mould and use language that's appropriate to the people you're talking to.

Directors and senior managers tend to converse in 'business speak' about 'helping to widen the margin', 'reducing the cost base', 'advancing the people agenda' and so on. You may feel that the best way to integrate your message into their business outlook is to talk to them in the same terms. On the other hand, frontline managers and employees tend to prefer plain English and will switch off if you use too much jargon.

Being savvy

Understanding how organisations work is important. For example, it's optimistic – or naïve – to go to an operations meeting and expect to get all members of the meeting (including the boss) to agree to something that you present for the first time. You have to prepare the ground carefully.

Playing 'dot-to-dot' in this way is vital – while going round talking through and selling the idea to each person individually may take time, it'll give you the opportunity to build into your proposal countermeasures to their concerns before they're aired at the meeting. You can maintain the credibility of your suggestions and also build on your relationship with the people you're working with.

It's also worth thinking about what the counterarguments are likely to be when you meet the people you want to influence. If you can think of them beforehand and have your answers ready, so much the better.

Attitude

A common response from people who don't want to do something is that the safety professional doesn't know how the operation works in the real world. Therefore, if you start off by telling them what to do, the barriers will come up instantly. If you've come to safety after some time spent doing something else, you may be able to empathise with this attitude. But many safety practitioners these days enter the profession as their first career choice, and in your zeal to improve safety, it's easy to forget that staff have other priorities as well as safety.

One of the best ways to overcome this challenge is to be honest. Make it clear to your audience that you realise they're the experts in what they do but that you're the specialist in health and safety. You need to work together to make the most of each other's expertise.

Concentrate first on the things you can agree on. Most of the things operational staff want to do to get their job done will be fine from a health and safety point of view. It's normally only a small element that will need a little more work to make it acceptable to both parties.

Not my job!

At some point someone will say that health and safety is not their job – they don't need to do it because the organisation has a safety professional. While you know why this view is wrong, you probably won't get very far by explaining the employees' duties section of the Health and Safety at Work etc. Act. As we've seen, talking about the law is guaranteed to turn your audience off.

The best solution is to explain it in context. One safety professional I knew did this very well with an operations manager who was objecting to doing risk assessments. The safety professional asked: "When you leave your company car, do you lock it?"

To which the operations manager replied: "Yes, of course I do."

"So you don't get a security guard to do it because it's really a security issue?"

"Don't be silly!"

"Well, the same thing applies to health and safety."

Admitting defeat

It may not be positive thinking, but it's true that sometimes, despite your best efforts, you can't overcome inaction. If the blockage is at middle management level or lower you can, of course, go higher up the management chain for support – but what happens if that support isn't forthcoming? You've identified the real problem, but what then? Even getting your boss involved may still not sort things out. In the end you have two choices: either call time and move on, or keep your head down and battle away.

The first option is the easy way out for sure – just pity the next person that comes along. The second choice is not for the faint hearted. But if you do stay, remember to put things in writing because when things go wrong (and in an organisation with these characteristics they will – it's just a matter of time) you need to be able to defend yourself. Organisations that don't take health and safety seriously tend to use the safety professional as the 'whipping boy' far more than those that take it seriously.

Conclusion

Using legal and moral obligations as a starting point for safety arguments is reactive in that you're encouraging action through fear of the consequences if something goes wrong. On the other hand, making strong cases for action based on commercial benefit is proactive and allows all parties to get what they want. Commercial benefit is also of particular interest to senior management teams.

Traditional arguments only win a certain number of people over. You need to have other ways to deal with inaction, crucially by thinking differently and applying your thinking creatively. Most of the time, people won't disagree that there's a problem, but they may disagree with the solution.

It's important to learn to pick your fights. Most of the time, as long as the problem is dealt with, does it matter whether your solution is used? If other people in the organisation come up with their own solution, it shows they're taking ownership of health and safety management. You only need to fight the small minority of problems where you fundamentally disagree with the solution the organisation has chosen, as you don't think it'll deal with the problem.

Chapter 9: Getting directors' attention and keeping it

It's been known for a long time that the commitment of an organisation's leadership to health and safety is critical to its success. This is one of the five key factors cited by the Confederation of British Industry in *Developing a safety culture: business for safety*.[12] It was also one of the major themes running through the report of the committee Lord Robens chaired, which formed the basis of the Health and Safety at Work etc Act 1974 (see Chapter 1). But how can you achieve it?

If a director talks with conviction and passion about health and safety, he or she will probably have a more powerful effect on advancing an organisation's safety culture than any safety professional is likely to be able to achieve in a whole career. There's a simple reason for this: if it's important to the boss, it gets done. Therefore, it's essential to get health and safety on directors' agendas.

Although you may spend a great deal of time and effort focusing your attention on the organisation's top level of management, it's generally worth it. These are the organisation's most powerful people – if you can get them on side, your life will be easier.

There are some unique characteristics about a director's role in an organisation that sets them apart from other members of a senior management team. The Institute of Directors' fact sheet[13] on the subject defines them as:

- providing leadership for the organisation
- determining the future of the organisation and its ethics as well as protecting its assets and reputation
- considering the organisation's stakeholders in their decision making (see Chapter 2)
- taking ultimate responsibility for the long-term prosperity of the organisation
- being accountable to the organisation's shareholders for overall performance.

In short, they deal with high level and other strategic issues rather than getting involved in the detail. In the health and safety context, they probably don't want to know what the organisation's approach is to managing vehicle movements on its sites, but they do need to know that it has one. This sounds obvious, but it's surprising how many safety professionals go into unnecessary detail when dealing with this audience. Unfortunately, this has the opposite effect to that intended and turns their attention off instead of engaging them.

With the increasing importance of corporate governance, and more recently the introduction of the Corporate Manslaughter and Corporate Homicide Act 2007, more and more directors want not only to do the right thing, but to be seen to be doing the right thing as well. You could argue, therefore, that the challenge for the modern safety professional is not getting directors' attention – it's maintaining their interest. This chapter outlines some best practice tools to help get directors' attention and keep it.

Board steering group

Most board meetings will contain an element of health and safety, even if it's just as simple as seeing the organisation's safety performance for the period. For many years, safety professionals argued that this wasn't enough, and in 2007 this was recognised by the Health and Safety Commission and the Institute of Directors, which published joint guidance[14] on the leadership actions that directors and board members can take on health and safety at work. The guidance suggests that setting up a board steering group is a good idea, but how do you do it?

The steering group is a subset of the main board and has the same standing orders and similar terms of reference as other subcommittees. Its aim is to maintain the impetus on health and safety matters at the senior levels of the organisation.

As each organisation is set up differently, it's difficult to suggest who exactly should sit on the steering group. The following list is a good starting point, along with a safety professional:

- operations director (chair)
- HR director
- sales director
- finance manager
- property manager
- a regional manager (or two)
- a senior representative from the organisation's insurers.

Operations director

Typically, the operations director is responsible for the money-making side
of the business. This is also the part of the business with the most staff
and often with the most health and safety risk.

HR director

Most organisations delegate health and safety responsibilities to the HR
director, and there are good reasons for this. He or she is independent of
the operational line and holds a leadership position. Health and safety in
the workplace should also form an integral part of the organisation's
'people agenda'. Clearly, directors with this sort of responsibility would
not want to find themselves marginalised by not being involved with the
steering group.

Sales director

At first sight, this may seem a strange addition to a steering group for
health and safety. But consider that the sales team are the people who go
out and win business – is health and safety taken into account when
setting up the pricing structure for the contract? Or do operational
colleagues have to correct the problem afterwards while working within
the margins agreed by the sales team? There are other powerful reasons
for the sales director to be involved. Not only are they in charge of people,
but also they're perfectly placed to make the most of the competitive
advantage that can be obtained by excelling in safety.

Finance manager

Finance tends to be another function in an organisation that is forgotten
in relation to health and safety management. But at this level some buy-in
from the finance team is important – they need to see the bigger picture of
the work involved before they'll be willing to allocate scarce resources.

Property manager

A lot of health and safety problems come down to building and equipment
issues. It can sometimes be difficult to explain this to board members – the
steering group provides an opportunity to do so.

Regional manager

The steering group has a great deal of potential to advance the safety
culture of an organisation, but it can be in danger of 'ivory tower'
syndrome – the perception that its members are making decisions without
referring to the staff on the ground who actually do the work. Involving
one or two regional managers can help counter this. The regional
managers involved will undoubtedly start to be safety champions among

their peers when they see just how seriously safety is taken at the top. It's also a good opportunity for succession planning and development by giving them exposure to a different part of the organisation and showing their talent to members of the organisation's leadership.

Senior representative from the insurers

It's nice to get approval from an external source saying: "Yes, I think you're going in the right direction." If approached, most employers' liability insurers will provide someone with the relevant background to do this. As well as assuring the organisation that it's going in the right direction, involving an insurer's representative allows you to benefit from the best practice the insurer has learnt from other clients. Insurers often welcome this kind of involvement, too, as it allows them to gather feedback from their customers.

Safety professional

The role of the safety professional in this steering group is similar to the one he or she performs at a safety committee, but at a much higher level. You may need to be more prepared and polished, but the rewards include getting directors and other influential people in the organisation to champion your cause.

The mechanics of the steering group

Once the steering group has been established, it needs some terms of reference. Here are some ideas:

- review the previous period's safety performance
- review and agree the next period's activities
- identify and remove existing blocks to improving safety performance
- support the development of the safety strategy
- update the main board and champion safety issues at its meetings.

How often the steering group meets will depend on how much there is to talk about, but given that it's dealing with strategic issues, once a quarter is probably enough. That said, an emergency meeting may sometimes be required – for example, to discuss a Prohibition Notice that's been issued or to form a major accident review panel that looks at the outcome of a serious incident investigation.

It's important to maintain momentum. You can do this by bringing in different external speakers to address the steering group. It's important, though, to pick your speakers so that they're relevant to the rest of the agenda.

For example, you may want to launch a driver safety training programme in the next six months, for which you'll need funds. An external speaker who can sell the virtues of this kind of investment can be very useful, particularly if he or she can get the group's enthusiasm fired up. Not only will this help you to get the funding you need, but your invited speaker will be able to talk to other people in the organisation about what's coming up and why it's important.

High level safety performance

There are many different ways to report safety performance and each organisation has its own tools for doing so. There are two common problems with providing the board with safety performance data. Either they see a load of figures that mean little to them, or they get too much detail, which they don't have time to read. Obviously, finding a happy medium is important, but it can also be difficult.

It's often better to provide a small number of measures that people really understand and can relate to. We suggest sticking to four key performance indicators:

- your organisation's RIDDOR rate
- its severity rate
- its accident reporting ratio
- the tripwire audit results.

RIDDOR rate

Using your organisation's incidence rate of RIDDOR-reportable accidents is handy as it allows the organisation to compare itself to the rest of British industry and specifically to the rest of its sector. Official figures are provided by the HSE and the Office for National Statistics. You'll probably find it helpful to recalculate the rates provided by HSE, though: using a multiplier of 1,000 rather than the HSE's 100,000 will make more sense to your board unless you work for a very large organisation.

Severity rate

This is a measure of how bad accidents are, as it measures the time injured parties have off work as a result. The higher the rate, the more time off is taken and thus the higher the cost to the business.

Accident reporting ratio

All too often, organisations restrict their focus to declining accident rates. Of course this is important, but there must be a measure of assurance that the number of accidents reported is a true reflection of what is going on.

In other words, is everything being reported? If not, you're living in a fool's paradise.

The simplest way to assess the number of incidents is to determine the number of RIDDOR-reportable accidents involving employees and express it as a ratio of the number of minor accidents reported in the same period. Then compare that ratio to an accepted 'accident triangle', such as the one noted in the HSE's publication *Successful health and safety management* (HSG65).[9] Here is a worked example:

Worked example of an accident reporting ratio. The shortfall between actual and target results suggests there may be a problem with underreporting of minor accidents

No. of RIDDOR-reportable accidents	No. of minor accidents reported	Actual reporting ratio	Target reporting ratio
7	35	1 : 5	1 : 7

Tripwire audit results
In Chapter 7, we outlined the concept of a tripwire audit. To balance the reactive data above, the board members should get proactive data as well to allow them to see the whole picture. In this case it may be the number of obvious high-risk safety issues identified but not yet effectively managed, both for the period and the year to date.

Ultimately, these measures should provide enough detail for the board's purposes, because all they need to know is how well the risks associated with the organisation are being managed and what is being done about them. If they have any questions or they want clarification, they'll tell you.

League tables
Introducing competition between functions or operational divisions by comparing and ranking their performance is something that many organisations do. If you're thinking of going down this route, be careful, as there can be some unintended side-effects:

- it can foster a culture of under-reporting, making it increasingly important to monitor reporting rates
- regional or departmental managers may start to argue about every accident, which distracts your attention from other areas of your work.

Management system ownership
As mentioned previously, organisations usually nominate one director to be responsible for making sure the health and safety policy is implemented. If this is perceived wrongly, it may encourage other members

of the board to rest on their laurels, thinking that health and safety is 'someone else's problem'. It's obviously essential to get everyone interested in seeing that the health and safety policy works.

One best practice way round this is for the managing director to retain overall responsibility for health and safety, but to give each director specific health and safety policies to 'own'. This approach is suggested in the HSC's publication, *Directors' responsibilities for health and safety*.[14] The table below takes this suggestion and gives some examples of which aspects of the health and safety management system could be owned by which director.

HR director	Operations director
• Misuse of drugs and alcohol • Shift working • Young people • New and expectant mothers • Disability • Stress	• Risk assessment • Workplace transport • COSHH • Electricity • Access • Fire
Finance director (where he or she is responsible for building maintenance) • Contractor management • Legionnaire's disease	Marketing director • Communication • Signs and signals
IT director • Computer workstations	Sales director • Occupational road risk

Examples of how management system elements can be allocated to different directors

For this type of approach to work, the managing director has to be willing to oversee the whole process. The way the management system is divided between directors' needs to reflect each director's area of responsibility, and there must be a highly visible safety team to support it.

This approach doesn't remove the need for safety professionals. In fact, it raises their profile immensely: not only do they write the policies (with other relevant stakeholders), but to make the approach successful they have to work with all of the directors. In older management structures, on the other hand, they tend to report to one board member alone.

This approach isn't for the faint hearted. It will only work when the senior management commitment to health and safety is already there and the organisation has started to show evidence of an advanced positive safety culture.

Cost control

Business is based on the principle of an organisation selling goods or services to others at a higher rate than it costs them to sell or provide them. The difference is the profit margin and organisations are always looking at ways to widen their margins. This can be done through sourcing cheaper raw materials or running a more efficient operation with a smaller cost base.

Health and safety is often seen as a function that wants to spend money without offering anything tangible in return. But there are opportunities for safety professionals to help their organisation to widen its margins, through providing opportunities to deliver cost savings.

Identifying costs

The first step in helping to widen the margin is to determine how much the current situation in health and safety is costing the business. There are lots of tools available to help determine the cost of incidents to the organisation, but the figure you end up with is always going to be an estimate, no matter how hard you try.

As part of the 'Revitalising health and safety' strategy, the HSE has carried out a great deal of work to help organisations identify how much workplace accidents cost them.[15] The HSE offers three relatively simple figures and one of these, from the HSE's own research, suggests that the cost of uninsured losses arising from accidents is about 10 times that of the insurance premium. However, while this might suffice as a quick rule of thumb, directors are likely to want an approach to costing that is more tailored to the organisation's particular circumstances.

In the same programme, the HSE developed an incident cost calculator, which helps to quantify in more detail the cost of an incident. For smaller companies, it may be practical to complete the tool for each incident, although this may not be practical for larger organisations. Nevertheless, the information needed for the HSE's tool is still valid. The trick is to work out the cost of known incidents and use estimates where necessary.

Once you've identified the cost of the incidents, it's important to put that into the context of the margin. In other words, you need to show, based on current margins, the amount of turnover needed to recoup the losses made as a result of incidents. Here is a worked example:

In 2008, a national clothing retailer reported 80 injuries and dangerous occurrences under RIDDOR and recorded 900 non-reportable incidents.

During the year, the company was working on a 10 per cent profit margin. Given that the estimated cost of incidents for the period was £1.5 million, the company would have had to generate £15 million-worth of sales to pay for the incidents alone, as shown in the summary below.

Total incident costs	£1.5 million
Margin	10 per cent
Turnover needed to recoup incident costs	£15 million

Managing costs and focusing minds

Identifying the scale of the financial benefits to improving safety performance is important and helps to get people's attention, but there are other ways in which you can help widen the margin. The following suggestions are best-practice examples linked to managing insurance-related costs.

Claims modelling

Most, if not all, organisations will have an excess on their public and employer's liability insurance – this is also known as the self-insured element. This can vary greatly and organisations can end up paying large amounts of money to claimants if it's experiencing numerous claims which individually fall below the excess. This expense is, of course, on top of the existing premiums.

Claims modelling is a well-used technique for analysing the organisation's claims experience to determine what types of accident are likely to result in a successful claim. This works well where organisations have a high volume claims experience.

Experience shows that when the claims experience is examined, the trends will centre, among other things, on the claimant's workplace, the amount of time off, whether there were any witnesses to the incident and the injury type. Once this information is known, all accident reports that come in are compared to these criteria and, if they match, they're rigorously investigated, irrespective of the accident's outcome. This creates three distinct advantages:

- A file can be compiled with a full incident investigation carried out by a safety professional, including photos, witness statements and the like taken as close to the time of the accident as possible. This procedure overcomes many of the common reasons why claims are difficult to defend.

- If the person involved in the incident is 'trying it on', he or she is less likely to consider putting a claim in if he or she thinks the organisation has the evidence it needs to defend itself. This doesn't affect genuine claimants who are injured as a result of their employer's negligence, who rightly deserve compensation.
- The information gathered in this way helps the organisation to make an accurate and informed decision on liability.

Recharging

Many organisations place an internal charge on a site's or department's profit and loss account for any successful health and safety-related claim. While this charge is unlikely even to cover the administrative cost of the claim, it does help focus the site manager's attention on the need to manage health and safety effectively, as it hurts him or her in the pocket – particularly if his or her bonus is related to profit and loss performance – while keeping the money in the organisation.

Premium contribution

Another successful technique used by a number of organisations is to apportion insurance premium contributions to different departments or units based on their claims history, rather than taking it out of the central pot, where either nobody feels the pinch or everyone pays the same. Again, this approach helps to keep people focused on the need to manage health and safety effectively.

It may not be immediately obvious why the issue of recharging and premium contribution are matters for directors' engagement. But they are likely to be radical changes from the existing arrangements and will probably have far-reaching ramifications. Also, you'll need to have the approval of senior management if you're to succeed in implementing them.

External recognition

As we discussed in Chapter 1, health and safety doesn't have to be all doom and gloom. Getting recognised for managing it effectively is something worth shouting about and plenty of opportunities exist to do both.

Organisations can be recognised externally by independent bodies for their safety performance or the programmes they've implemented. This sort of recognition is great and its effects go beyond the awards dinner and the chance for a director to stand up and accept the award. Awards and recognition are also another example of how the safety professional can add value to the business by helping to deliver competitive advantage – does any other organisation in your sector have that award?

Conclusion

As a sector of the workforce, directors are the most influential in any organisation. The importance of getting them on side can't be overstated.

When considering how to get them involved and lead health and safety, you need to remember that they're extremely busy people. The tools discussed in this chapter are deliberately simple, but they do require director-level involvement to make them successful.

They also give directors tangible tasks that they need to do to lead health and safety in the organisation.

Chapter 10: Middle management – getting the sandwich filling right

In the previous chapter we discussed various ways to help engage directors and senior managers in an organisation. One thing is certain: once this group of people has been switched on to health and safety, they'll push the wave through the business.

This wave will invariably hit the middle managers who report direct to them first, but so does everything else on the directors' agenda – sales, working capital, widening the margin, achieving customer service level agreements or employee retention rates. And the pressure on middle managers doesn't just come from on high; they get it from below as well. They're the buffer (or sandwich filling) between senior management and the sharp end.

In some organisations it seems that everyone has 'manager' in their job title, yet a lot of these 'managers' are not managers. Typically, a manager has similar areas of responsibility as a director but in a smaller (or more local) area. They tend to be more aware of the details, and have well-defined problem-solving and people management skills.

It's important to remember all this when finding ways to engage them, because you'll be competing with many other people and functions for their attention – and they all think their area is more important than the next. Successfully engaging this group of people comes down to having their boss on side, breaking things down into manageable chunks, making things snappy, and building on existing systems and processes.

The middle manager's job is not an easy one; he or she has to deliver the performance demanded by the board in challenging circumstances where no two locations they're responsible for are likely to be the same. For these reasons, middle management is arguably one of the hardest groups of the organisational population to engage. This chapter gives some best practice examples of how to get them involved and engaged with health and safety, and follows the engagement model shown on the next page. The model is based on the need to have a highly visible and supportive safety professional and works on the assumption that senior management support is available.

The engagement strategy has three critical elements:

- providing safety training that's aimed at the right level for the audience
- using active and reactive monitoring data
- using performance management techniques to drive performance.

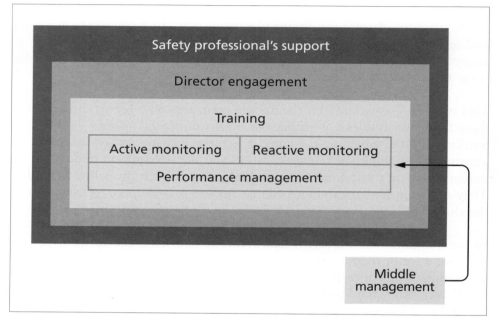

A health and safety engagement strategy model for middle managers

Safety training

Providing safety training always tends to be the first thing on a safety professional's agenda and it's a necessary part of an engagement strategy. But remember that the course is only part of the training (see Chapter 6) – it needs to be linked to a well-considered development programme. That said, what kind of course is most suitable to provide the necessary basic knowledge? It can be very difficult to choose because there are so many different options available.

In-house courses have the advantage of being automatically tailored to the needs of the organisation. But they do sometimes lack the credibility of having an external trainer to deliver the message (particularly if you choose the right provider – see Chapter 6). Remember too that someone else will deliver an external course for you, leaving you to concentrate on other things.

When choosing an external course, the key is to think about your audience. While every organisation has its own requirements, middle managers in general tend to fall into three broad categories, as the examples on the next page show.

It's also not uncommon for managers of this level to gain a formal health and safety qualification, such as the NEBOSH General Certificate.

This kind of training will undoubtedly benefit the learner, but it's important to understand that by themselves they're not the solution to achieving the engagement you're looking for.

Ideally, the right kind of training with a good trainer will stimulate the learners enough for them to want to find out more or to change their behaviour to improve the safety culture in their area of the organisation. But this will all be lost if the training isn't backed up by a wider health and safety strategy which requires some positive action from the managers.

It's essential to capitalise on the impact of the training, otherwise all the money you have spent will be wasted – use the managers' new-found knowledge or lose it!

Health and safety objective

It's common practice for organisations to give their employees objectives (often related to their bonus) over and above their normal routine tasks, or that aim to 'raise the bar' by stretching their current performance.

Most organisations' bonus schemes are awarded against organisational performance and the completion of individual objectives. Their aim is simple – to motivate people to perform at the highest level they can. While they get recognition and a financial reward, the organisation reaps the benefits of their work – everybody wins. The use of bonus schemes is based on well-known and recognised psychological theories related to positive and negative reinforcement... and greed.

There's an opportunity in all this for the safety professional to exploit the existing arrangements and get health and safety included in the objective-setting process. If done correctly, this will really help achieve engagement with the target population.

If you're not convinced, find out what's on your organisation's objective list for middle management. The chances are that it's these objectives that the managers talk about and work towards most of the time – precisely because they're set as objectives. But you need to plan this kind of

Example 1	
Manager group	Area managers
Organisation type	Specialist food retailer
Role outline	Responsible for all trading activities for 15–20 stores across a geographically defined area, reporting to a regional manager
Course	IOSH *Safety for senior executives*
Justification	The course is aimed at managers who need to understand the implications of their decisions in relation to health and safety, and need to develop or understand a safety strategy. The course lasts only one day, making it easier for this group of managers to find the time to attend

Example 2	
Manager group	Operational managers (production, engineering, distribution)
Organisation type	Food and drink manufacturing
Role outline	Responsible for a defined part of the manufacturing site and process and its operations. They report to the site general manager and have a number of team leaders between them and front-line staff. Work activities tend to be higher risk
Course	IOSH *Managing safely*
Justification	This four- or five-day course covers the fundamental elements needed to manage safety effectively and teaches how to carry out risk assessments and accident investigations as well as monitoring techniques

Example 3	
Manager group	Non-operational managers
Organisation type	Any
Role outline	Typically responsible for support aspects of the business (eg HR, marketing, finance) and managing large teams of people
Course	IOSH *Safety for senior executives*
Justification	As in example 1, this course is aimed at managers who need a quick overview of their responsibilities so that they have the knowledge necessary to consider health and safety in their decisions

programme carefully. Done right, they have great potential, but if they're poorly implemented, they'll lose credibility and be talked about as an example of how not to do it for years to come.

The acronym SMART is well understood these days when talking about objective setting – objectives need to be Specific, Measurable, Agreed (with the people responsible for meeting the objective), Realistic (stretching but achievable) and Time-bound (ie with a timescale for completion). Yet when you're setting objectives you can meet the criteria of SMART and still get it wrong. Many organisations link part of middle managers' bonuses to the health and safety performance of the part of the business they're responsible for. Unfortunately, the objective tends to be linked to accident performance, for example: 'In 2009 achieve a lost-time incident frequency rate of X.' There are three problems associated with this type of objective:

- it can lead to a culture of under-reporting
- it's a reactive measure and often down to luck – although it can be said in general that if managers control risks effectively they'll achieve a reduction in the number of accidents, in reality the connection can be too tenuous to be fair
- it can take attention away from sensible risk management – in other words, managers spend too much time looking at serious but unlikely potential accidents rather than trying to stop the more common but minor ones, which in any case are often key to preventing the serious ones.

A SMART objective which overcomes these problems would give the manager more of an incentive to be proactive as well as allowing them more control of their own destiny (achieving the bonus). The most obvious one is linked to the tripwire audit discussed in Chapter 7 and could be worded: "In 2009 achieve X per cent average score on the tripwire audits at the locations you're responsible for."

Linking an objective used in setting the bonus to active monitoring also reinforces the positive message that it pays to get out of your office and actively manage the situation.

Incident peer reviews
Often the details of accidents go below the radar of middle managers. Instead, they tend to focus on the numbers. This is understandable, given the way that many organisations and their bonus structures are set up.

But consider how powerful a statement it would make for a middle manager to start talking to injured employees about their accidents and asking questions of their direct reports about what could be done to prevent a similar recurrence. It positively affects the safety culture because the manager will think: "I'd better do this properly because the gaffer will want to know what I've done", but it also emphasises the personal aspect of accidents – they're not just numbers.

Incident peer reviews are a best-practice example which builds on these ideas. They can be used at site, departmental or organisational level and are probably best explained in the form of a worked example.

UK Parcels plc is a large parcel delivery business, employing 3,000 people who operate a central processing site and a network of 40 local delivery and collection depots across the UK. The local centres are split into 10 areas, each managed by an area manager who reports to the operations director.

At the end of each reporting period, all the details of the incidents that occurred during the period are sent out to all the area managers. A week later, either at a management meeting or via a conference call chaired by the operations director, some of the incidents are discussed. Those discussed are chosen at random by the operations director, who asks the relevant area manager to:

• explain what happened
• outline what steps have been taken to prevent it happening again
• say whether the accident affects the wider business.

To help the operations director, UK Parcels' safety professional is on hand to coach and guide the area managers in the right direction. The session is snappy and lasts no longer than 45 minutes.

How will this get area managers engaged? Consider it from the unengaged area manager's point of view – someone who hasn't prepared the details needed for the peer review meeting. They'll only fail to do it once, because they won't want to look foolish in front of their peers again, and they certainly won't want to show their boss (who is chairing the session) that they haven't done it, as it would become a performance management issue to be raised in their next one-to-one meeting.

Performance management

Every manager should be aware of the concept of performance management. It involves line managers making sure that their teams deliver the required results, and it works at all levels of an organisation.

The mechanisms for performance management are generally well established, and there's great advantage to be gained if they can be exploited in relation to health and safety. Here's another fictional case study to explain this best practice concept.

Philips Clothing is a high street retailer specialising in clothing for the 18–30 age market. Their 126 nationwide stores are split into 10 areas, each managed by an area manager. The area management team is then split into two regional teams (north and south), reporting to a regional business director.

The company uses a system of 'model' risk assessments based on worst case scenarios. Store managers are expected to review each assessment regularly and make sure that:

• the assessments are as store-specific as they need to be
• the findings are implemented.

The process for making sure this happens is built into the existing performance management system. The area managers visit each of the stores they're responsible for every month. Part of the discussion with the store managers is about health and safety, and particularly how far they've got with implementing the results of the risk assessments. If they're on track, it's fine – the area manager says "Well done, keep it up"; if not, the area manager offers support to the store manager to improve performance. If store managers are repeatedly 'off course', extra steps can be taken through the organisation's performance management or disciplinary framework.

This process is mirrored by the regional business director, who has one-to-one meetings with the area management team. The tripwire audit (see Chapter 7) can provide an alternative and independent picture. The diagram on the next page shows the overall process.

The idea of making health and safety a performance management issue is to get managers to relate to the subject on a practical level, and to make the link between health and safety and their job role stronger. Remember, though, that it's essential to establish that performance management is as

A simplified health and safety performance management system in schematic form

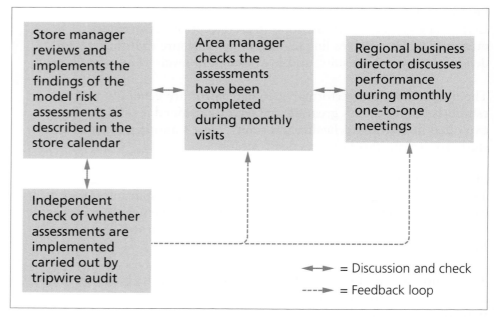

much about saying "Well done, great job" as it is about wielding the big stick.

Conclusion
None of the above is rocket science – far from it. Engaging middle managers is only as difficult as you make it. The thing to remember is that you don't need them to do lots of things. It's far better to ask them to do a handful of essential tasks very well.

Chapter 11: Employee engagement

Directors and managers have a great deal of influence over an organisation's safety performance and culture, but they don't tend to be the ones that have the accidents. It's the front-line employees that are most at risk and this is hardly surprising since they are the ones at the sharp end. Therefore, any safety engagement strategy that doesn't include this group would be fundamentally flawed.

At a basic level, it can be said that, providing the plant and equipment is safe for use and people follow the rules, accidents won't happen. Of course, in theory this is true, but life is rarely that simple. The question is how do you get people to follow the rules all the time, including when the boss isn't around to watch them?

The Health and Safety at Work etc Act promotes employee engagement through the duties of employees, as noted in Sections 7 and 8. But while these sections contain the threat of legal action against employees, you'd have to be very unlucky to be prosecuted. For employees, a more visible deterrent to not working safely is their contract of employment, backed up by the organisation's disciplinary policy. Many organisations treat major health and safety breaches as serious enough to warrant summary dismissal.

There's a place for 'sticks' such as this but there need to be some 'carrots' too. Choosing the right carrots has other benefits: as well as improving safety performance, they can help advance the organisation's wider people agenda.

There's a huge variety of workers in a wide range of industries, so it's impossible to list every engagement strategy which could be used. Instead, this chapter presents a number of best practice engagement methodologies that have been used across a broad range of industry sectors. All of them build on one of the main themes of this book: to break things down into manageable chunks.

The traditional approach
The first step in achieving employee ownership of your safety policy is to start a dialogue between the organisation and its staff. This mechanism has been established for a long time in the legal framework – not only in

the Health and Safety at Work etc Act but also in specific legislation (the Safety Representatives and Safety Committee Regulations 1977 and the Health and Safety (Consultation with Employees) Regulations 1996).

The problem with the traditional safety committee approach is that it can end up in a situation where people waffle for an hour or two once a month, have a pop at the management team and focus on more trivial issues. The net result: the important things get missed and safety takes another knock.

That said, safety committees and other consultation mechanisms are extremely important. The basic principles underlying them are valid and the remainder of this chapter will explain how to build on these principles to produce more forward-thinking strategies.

Safety champion programme

Good safety representatives will work with the organisation and the staff they represent to improve workplace standards. Unfortunately, the decline of unionised businesses over the last few decades has tended to reduce the number and effectiveness of safety representatives.

The safety champion programme is a variation on the safety representative concept. Its primary aim is to provide the frontline manager with another pair of hands to help them manage safety at their location. The precise details of safety champions' roles are, of course, for each individual organisation to determine, but common tasks include helping the local manager with:

- carrying out risk assessments
- supporting incident investigations
- challenging unsafe acts and conditions.

Getting the right safety champion is therefore critical. Just as for every other job, you need a job description and person specification. The person specification for the role might include the following attributes:

- reliability and trustworthiness
- being a team player and good at problem-solving
- approachability
- interest in health and safety
- respect from their peers for working safely.

There are two major differences between the safety champion role and the normal job of the person you choose as the champion. These need to be addressed from the beginning, as you won't get senior managers' support for the programme unless they are. These differences are that:

- the safety champion role is an extension of the person's existing job – he or she isn't the location's full-time health and safety person. That responsibility remains with the manager
- safety champions may not get paid any extra for doing the role.

Often, a criticism of organisations is that they continually dump new initiatives on frontline managers and expect them to implement them despite their existing workloads. This programme helps to overcome this, by providing help for the already busy location manager in managing safety in their workplace at little additional cost.

You may also find resistance to a safety champion programme because people think that the role will take safety champions away from their 'day job' for too long, with a cost to the organisation. But in reality, the safety champion role is only likely to require about half an hour a week of the person's time away from their normal work. In the broader scheme of things, this isn't much, particularly if it frees up some time for the manager to do other tasks.

While safety champions may not get paid any more for performing these additional duties, there does need to be some form of incentive for them. Some organisations offer a small addition to the salary, in much the same way as they do for first aiders. But there are other selling points for the role:

- they will receive training (which, depending on the training course, could be accredited by a professional body)
- the programme allows people to get onto the first rung of the safety profession's career ladder
- it provides an opportunity to showcase their potential and talent outside their normal field of work
- it gives them the chance to make a difference to improve workplace safety for themselves and their colleagues.

It would be counterproductive to put someone in post without giving them any training. As we discussed in previous chapters, there's plenty of choice in this area. IOSH's *Managing safely* course will fit the bill in many cases, but in-house training based on the specific tasks required of the safety champions may work equally well, at least in the first instance. You may find that, as their practical experience increases, your safety champions become interested in a more in-depth course, which you could use as a reward for meeting safety objectives.

Once your safety champions have been trained, it's important to make sure that they have some direction so that they know what they're doing when they go back to the workplace. You can't just leave them to it – it's important that you, as the safety professional, keep in touch with them and support them when they need it.

Once you've appointed several safety champions, you can set up a safety champion network. The safety champions can use this to support each other as well as coming together to discuss wider safety programmes and challenges at regular intervals – perhaps twice a year.

This programme has the potential to work well in all workplaces. The key tasks to carry out when putting it in place are to:

- gain organisational support
- determine budget constraints
- agree a job description and person specification
- recruit and select suitable champions
- identify a training provider
- give training
- determine, in conjunction with the location manager, specific tasks for the champions to do in their workplace
- introduce personal development plans for safety champions linked to their main plan
- maintain regular contact
- offer refresher training as necessary.

Risk assessment working group

Often, one of the weak points with risk assessments is that they tend to be written in isolation by safety professionals – not only do safety professionals see them as a core part of their job, but the organisation often takes this view too. This means that the recommendations for controlling the risks identified may be written from a purely theoretical health and safety point of view and may not reflect the way the job is really done or the local challenges that mean the job can't be done as prescribed.

Although this traditional approach lets the organisation put a tick in the box that says 'risk assessments completed', there's a high chance that the safety professional will fail to get any engagement from the workforce and that the assessments won't be meaningful. But is engagement necessary with risk assessment? The answer is clearly yes, because without it the recommendations may not be followed. After all, managers enforcing the rules will only get you so far, and to improve results you'll need to have the goodwill of the staff who are actually doing the work.

The following best practice example aims to make sure that risk assessments are done, that their recommendations are implemented and managed by the people that do the job, and that they're still OK from a safety point of view.

The concept is simple. Form a risk assessment team, made up of members of the workforce from all departments, eg production, engineering, distribution. You can select each department's representative by using a similar person specification as for the safety champion programme. Give all the representatives training in general risk assessment techniques and then ask them, in pairs, to carry out various assessments from your list of assessments that need doing.

Every few weeks, bring the group together to review the assessments they've completed. You can then sign off the recommendations from a safety professional's point of view (eg for technical accuracy) and get the approval of a senior manager – someone who can authorise expenditure, agree safety rules for the location, and make sure people are trained in the necessary safe systems of work.

It's vital that you as the safety professional attend these review meetings, as the following case study shows.

A member of a risk assessment team presented an assessment following an incident to consider the task of moving two roll cages at the same time. It was explained that the operative was pushing one cage while pulling the other. To prevent the following cage striking the operative's heels when they stopped suddenly, safety boots with steel toecaps and heel protection were required. On the face of it, this seemed perfectly reasonable and the site manager was about to tell someone in the procurement team to source the necessary footwear. However, best practice in this situation is that operatives should only move one cage at a time and that they should always push them – the only time a cage should be pulled is to manoeuvre it into a position where it can be pushed.

From the non-technical viewpoint, the manager's footwear solution seemed reasonable. The safety professional needed to be at the meeting to explain the technical best practice solution to the problem. Despite the shortcomings, this example does show that people are taking an interest in health and safety, and this should not be stifled.

If the team comes across an urgent health and safety problem that needs to be resolved before the next team meeting, they can put the problem and solutions in the form of a risk assessment and present it to a site manager, effectively saying: "Here is the problem and this is what we think we need to do about it."

Naturally, there will be areas where more specialist risk assessment training – or at least additional knowledge – will be required, for example when looking at chemical safety, manual handling and the like. In these cases, assessors from the main team should be given training to help them develop their specialist skills – these will help not just with health and safety but also in their normal job. For example, an engineer who attends a work equipment and machinery safety course will not only be able to consider whether there are any additional guarding requirements for a new machine being introduced in the factory, but will also be able to contribute to the working party looking at where to site the machine and how it can be used most efficiently.

This approach works very well where there are several higher risk activities going on at a single site, such as in a production and manufacturing environment. The key activities when putting this programme together are:

- getting site management support (using arguments like 'many hands make light work')
- identifying potential team members
- determining what risk assessments need to be done
- devising and delivering general risk assessment training
- assigning risk assessments to pairs of working group members
- playing a prominent role yourself during the first few weeks for coaching and guidance
- holding a risk assessment working group meeting to review the assessments and implement the findings.

Risk assessment focus groups for front-line managers

Many larger organisations, especially those which aren't production or manufacturing-based, use model or generic risk assessments. These are devised by safety professionals centrally and then provided to front-line managers to implement in their workplace and adapt as necessary to make them relevant to the specific site and hazards.

As we discussed in connection with the risk assessment working group, in this case it's possible to fall into the 'ivory tower' situation, where the people writing the assessments are too far removed from the activities under consideration. In other words, solutions that look good on paper may not translate well into practice in the workplace.

To improve engagement with frontline managers, and to find out whether there are ways to do things that suit the operation and the safety professional better, you can use another best practice programme of risk assessment focus groups made up of frontline managers.

These groups typically meet quarterly (but more or less frequently if necessary) with the safety professional to review the model assessments. This gives the managers the chance to say whether a given idea will work, may work or definitely won't work, and to make further suggestions that you may not have thought of. This approach, of course, ensures that the assessments are really meaningful, but it also encourages members of the focus group to promote them, as they were instrumental in putting them together.

By engaging them in the process, this is an incredibly simple but effective way of getting frontline managers more on side and thinking proactively. The key factors when implementing this programme are:

- choosing focus group members (using similar criteria to the person specification discussed in the safety champion programme)
- providing some form of risk assessment training so that the group's members understand the process and the concept of the hierarchy of risk control
- meeting to review and implement assessments.

Safety award programmes
Safety award programmes are implemented on the basis of psychological theory relating to reward and punishment. In a work context this means: "Do well and you'll be rewarded; don't do so well and you won't."

Some traditional safety professionals will argue that people get paid to work safely and will question whether we need to spend more time, money and effort on implementing an award programme for something they should already be doing.[16] While it's quite easy to see their point, this mindset is unlikely to get you very far in helping to improve your organisation's safety culture and performance.

Award programmes are very easy to implement. The first consideration is to choose which behaviours, conditions and performance criteria you intend to reward. Then you need to decide how to measure the achievements and what form the reward will take.

There are many options when it comes to what behaviours, conditions and performance criteria you want to reward. You may ask staff to nominate individuals for working especially safely, or you could choose the site or department with the fewest reportable or lost-time injuries in the last year, or you could use the audit score.

It doesn't matter what you decide to reward, providing it supports the organisation's safety strategy and is a valid measure of safety success. You need to avoid falling into a common trap with safety award programmes – they can breed a culture of under-reporting and blame, both of which need to be avoided in health and safety.

For a safety award programme to have the desired effect – in other words, for people to change their behaviour to work more safely and to deal with unsafe conditions – there has to be a clear incentive from the beginning. You'll need to agree a budget and publicise the programme – not just the awarding criteria but the prize as well – before you go live with it.

The following fictional examples help to illustrate some of the pitfalls and how to get it right.

Case study A

A major manufacturing company operating on a single site ran a programme that was designed to reward the team that had the fewest lost-time accidents (LTAs). The afternoon production team, which had three fewer LTAs than their nearest rivals, won. The team manager was rewarded with a two-week holiday to Cyprus – the logic of this was based on the assumption that the manager must have been managing effectively for the team to get the result that it did. But this reward failed to take into account that it wasn't just the manager who delivered the result – the team leaders and employees did their part too. Needless to say, the programme's reputation suffered as a result.

Case study B

An organisation with a number of call centres in the UK ran a programme based on the following criteria:

- all team members must have carried out their display screen equipment risk assessments in the last year
- at least one team member per team must have attended every site health and safety committee meeting in the last year
- the team must have received a score of at least 90 per cent on their work area safety inspection (carried out by the facilities department) in their last three inspections.

Of the 14 teams working in the call centre, eight met these criteria. Each member of the eight teams received high street shopping vouchers as a way of saying 'well done!' Everyone was a winner.

These programmes can work in all organisations provided that the basics are well thought out. The key parts of the process are to:

- decide what behaviours, conditions and performance you want to reinforce
- find a way to make everyone who qualifies feel special – don't just have one overall winner
- set a budget
- decide on the awarding criteria
- choose prizes that are relevant to the people you're trying to engage
- launch and publicise
- prepare the results
- make the awards and publicise.

Active training

This best practice example is based on a technique used in the automotive manufacturing industry and is a version of a standard toolbox talk programme. Once a month, a safety topic is prepared by the safety professional for frontline managers to deliver to their team by a given deadline.

The session is led by the manager and is a conversation based around a number of hazards related to one of the team's work activities. The team members are then asked to come up with ways of dealing with the hazards and working safely. The manager steers them through this process, using the guide provided by the safety professional. Once they've agreed on safe ways of working, all the team members sign up to them.

This isn't always an easy programme to implement. The challenge isn't preparing the material but getting frontline managers to facilitate an interactive learning session, particularly as to be truly successful they really need to have done some preparation beforehand. That said, the advantages are clear – the programme:

- encourages dialogue, as it is interactive both in the team and beyond it, as there'll be feedback to the safety professional
- focuses on implementing practical solutions
- promotes "we thought of that ..." ideals rather than "not thought of round here" resistance.

The key factors when implementing this programme are to:

- prepare at least six months' worth of session material
- develop managers so that they can encourage learning (this may involve working with your colleagues in the HR or training department)
- launch the scheme and pay attention to the feedback.

Conclusion

Frontline employees and their line managers are the third and final piece in any health and safety engagement strategy. Safety committees have only limited capacity to influence employee engagement, so other measures are needed.

The best practice examples presented in this chapter are all based on trying to make things easier by finding creative ways to get more people involved in health and safety by being masters of their own destiny – a feeling lots of people like.

Chapter 12: Conclusion

No organisation in its right mind wants to hurt people. They therefore want well-rounded, professional general business managers who specialise in health and safety to help them improve their safety performance and culture – not people with clipboards and cagoules!

The negative perception the public has of health and safety is actually quite useful. It should be used as the acid test for all your decisions as a safety professional – in other words, ask "Is what I'm doing sensible?" If it's not, don't do it!

And it's worth remembering that we don't actually have it too bad. While it may seem that there's a fair bit of red tape around these days, there's considerably less than there was before the Health and Safety at Work etc Act was introduced in 1974.

We must bear in mind that the profession is part of a much wider and larger community, which extends well beyond the traditional safety representative and safety regulator roles into the exciting and high profile world of corporate social responsibility. If you're prepared to get out of your silo, this new world holds many opportunities for you to develop personally, as well as for putting the safety message across in a much smarter way.

We should all be constantly trying to raise the bar in terms of our performance, attitude and skills sets – something that we're being encouraged to do by IOSH. By doing this, you can start on the journey to becoming a world-class safety professional, where undoubtedly the rewards are greater.

Getting there is easier than you might think. Sure, it's more than just being able to present well and learning to pick your fights; but if you haven't got the basics right, how can you ever hope to influence your customers, survive in the cut and thrust of big business and navigate through the politics that often comes with it?

For your organisation's safety culture to develop positively, the whole area of health and safety must become ingrained into how the organisation operates. In terms of getting the 'biggest bang for your buck', you could do worse than developing a safety strategy that has clear and strong links with the organisation's overall aims and objectives. That way, safety is seen as really being key to the organisation's success.

Having done this, you need to remember not to switch people off, and consider your customers in everything you do. Put yourself in their shoes and ask what information they need to look after their team or themselves. What do they have already, what do they need and how best can I give it to them? Crack this, and you're well on your way to having engagement.

There are many different ways to engage with the different parts of the organisation – you're almost spoilt for choice. But rather than jumping in and trying to be everything to everyone, stop and work out where you should be spending your time, money and effort in order to get the best result. In other words, think like a general business manager.

Inevitably, you'll come across people who don't want to do what you want them to. When you do, don't panic! This should be where you get the most enjoyment out of your job and where you add the most value – by engaging the unengaged. Rather than approaching the subject head-on with the same old arguments that they'll be anticipating, think outside the box.

When someone goes to see a counsellor, they spend a great deal of time trying to find out what 'barriers' the person has put up that stop them doing what they want to do. This is helpful when you come up against inaction in the health and safety arena, too. Spend some time with the person, understand what their frame of reference is and help remove the barriers. It might take a little time, but it's far easier than meeting a brick wall and never getting anywhere. Hopefully it's clear why this will have a far better effect than saying: "You must do it because if you don't, you'll be breaking the law."

In summary, health and safety shouldn't be about stopping anything. It should be about enabling activities to take place through finding different ways to do things safely with sensible risk management. Moving away from our traditional roots and becoming more commercially 'savvy' is critical if our profession is to survive and develop.

References

1   Lord Robens. *Safety and health at work: report of the committee 1970–72*, CMND 5034. London: HMSO, 1972.
2   HSE Books. *HSE Books 2008 catalogue*. Sudbury: HSE Books, 2008.
3   Stokes P. Health and safety flattens pancake race. *Daily Telegraph*, 5 February 2008. Available at www.telegraph.co.uk/news/uknews/1577530/Health-and-safety-flattens-pancake-race.html.
4   HSE. *Number of workplace injuries reported to all enforcing authorities by industry 1981–2007/08p*. Available at www.hse.gov.uk/statistics/history/histinj.xls.
5   HSE. *Principles of sensible risk management*. Available at www.hse.gov.uk/risk/principlespoints.htm.
6   Companies Act 2006, Ch 46. London: HMSO, 2006. Available at www.opsi.gov.uk/acts/acts2006/ukpga_20060046_en_1.
7   IOSH. *Making a difference – a basic guide to environmental management for OSH practitioners*. Wigston: IOSH, 2009. Available at www.iosh.co.uk/guidance.
8   Environmental Protection Act 1990, Ch 43. London: HMSO, 1990. Available at www.opsi.gov.uk/acts/acts1990/ukpga_19900043_en_1.
9   HSE. *Successful health and safety management*, HSG65. Sudbury: HSE Books, 1997.
10 British Standards Institution. *BS OHSAS 18001 Occupational health and safety*. London: BSI, 2007.
11 Health and Safety at Work etc Act 1974, Ch 37. London: HMSO, 1974. Available at www.opsi.gov.uk/RevisedStatutes/Acts/ukpga/1974/cukpga_19740037_en_1.
12 Confederation of British Industry. *Developing a safety culture: business for safety*. London: CBI, 1990.
13 Institute of Directors. *The key differences between directors and managers*. Available at www.iod.com/intershoproot/eCS/Store/en/pdfs/managers.pdf.
14 HSC. *Directors' responsibilities for health and safety*, INDG343. Sudbury: HSE Books, 2008. Available at www.hse.gov.uk/pubns/indg343.pdf.
15 HSE. *Reduce risks, cut costs*, INDG355. Sudbury: HSE Books, 2002. Available at www.hse.gov.uk/pubns/indg355.pdf.
16 Byrne R. SHP IOSH Awards 2008: Keep your eyes on the prize. *The Safety and Health Practitioner* online, available at www.shponline.co.uk/article.asp?pagename=archive&article_id=7371.

Index